Shipwrecks
in 100
OBJECTS

To dear Stuart.
A good friend, sadly missed, who would have loved to chat about this book.

Shipwrecks
in 100
OBJECTS

Stories of Survival, Tragedy, Innovation and Courage

Simon Wills

FRONTLINE
BOOKS

Shipwrecks in 100 Objects
STORIES OF SURVIVAL, TRAGEDY, INNOVATION AND COURAGE

First published in Great Britain in 2022 by Frontline Books
An imprint of Pen & Sword Books Ltd,
Yorkshire - Philadelphia

ISBN 978 1 52679 221 1

CIP data records for this title are available from the British Library

Pen & Sword Books Limited incorporates the imprints of Atlas, Archaeology, Aviation, Discovery, Family History, Fiction, History, Maritime, Military, Military Classics, Politics, Select, Transport, True Crime, Air World, Frontline Publishing, Leo Cooper, Remember When, Seaforth Publishing, The Praetorian Press, Wharncliffe Local History, Wharncliffe Transport, Wharncliffe True Crime and White Owl.

PEN & SWORD BOOKS LTD
47 Church Street, Barnsley, South Yorkshire, S70 2AS, England
E-mail: enquiries@pen-and-sword.co.uk
Website: www.pen-and-sword.co.uk

Or
PEN AND SWORD BOOKS
1950 Lawrence Rd, Havertown, PA 19083, USA
E-mail: Uspen-and-sword@casematepublishers.com

For more information on our books, please visit
www.frontline-books.com, email info@frontline-books.com
or write to us at the above address.

Printed and bound by CPI Group (UK) Ltd, Croydon, CR0 4YY.

Typeset in 10/14pt Adobe Caslon by SJmagic DESIGN SERVICES, India.

Contents

Acknowledgements

A book of this scale can only be achieved with the assistance of many other people. I'd particularly like to thank my partner, B, for his kindness and patience during the long period over which this book was written. Sarah Cook was the diligent copy editor for this book and I'm so grateful for her attention to detail. Martin Mace at Pen & Sword was also very generous with his advice, support and enthusiasm. Linne Matthews gave me great encouragement at the start which I really appreciated, and most of my friends have tolerated me talking incessantly about this book for quite a long time.

The archives that I have used for research include The National Archives, the National Maritime Museum (Greenwich), Southampton Maritime Library, the Imperial War Museum and the British Library. I'd like to thank all their staff for being organised and helpful to me.

I'm especially grateful to Jonathan Moore, Charles Dagneau and Aaron Skoblenick (Parks Canada); John Burland (Joseph Conrad Society); Duncan Bosworth (Australian Transport Safety Bureau); Ross Anderson and Teori Shannon (Western Australian Shipwrecks Museum); Helen Kibblewhite and Kirsty Parson (National Army Museum); Lucia Rinolfi (British Museum); and Mark Beattie-Edwards (Nautical Archaeology Society).

Image Credits

I am grateful to the following organisations and individuals for permission to use the images specified below:

Ch2, rosary found on board the carrack *Mary Rose*, by Peter Crossman of the Mary Rose Trust, [File: MaryRose-rosary-81A1414h.JPG] courtesy of Wikimedia Commons, under creative common Attribution-ShareAlike 3.0 Unported (CC BY-SA 3.0), https://creativecommons.org/licenses/by-sa/3.0/deed.en

Ch2, Wreckage of the Tudor warship *Mary Rose* on display in museum, seanseyeview/Shutterstock.com [stock photo ID 1334631893]

Ch3, Armada medal, Library of Congress Rare Book and Special Collections Division, The Hans P. Kraus Collection of Sir Francis Drake

Ch5, image of *Trial* cannon. Photo taken by the author, used here with kind permission of Western Australian Shipwrecks Museum, where the cannon is located

Ch7, sundial from *London*, © London Shipwreck Trust

Ch9, image of clam, by Pawelec, [File:Tridacna.JPG] courtesy of Wikimedia Commons, under creative common Attribution-ShareAlike 3.0 Unported (CC BY-SA 3.0), https://creativecommons.org/licenses/by-sa/3.0/deed.en

Ch12, image of Stede Bonnet, courtesy of Library of Congress Rare Book and Special Collections Division, Washington, USA

Ch13, title page and illustration from *Robinson Crusoe* (1719), held by the British Library and made available under a Public Domain Mark 1.0 licence.

Ch14, satellite image from Google Earth Pro, https://earth.google.com Imagery and data attribution: Google – Landsat/ Copernicus Data SIO, NOAA, U.S. Navy, NGA, GEBCO

Ch16, Medieval castle of Fougères in Brittany, Oliver Hoffmann/Shutterstock.com [stock photo ID 722342401]

Ch18, bowl and lid from Palau (image ID 00958306001) © Trustees of the British Museum. All rights reserved

Ch19, Lionel Lukin's design for a lifeboat, courtesy of the Wellcome Collection, https://wellcomecollection.org designated Creative Commons, Public Domain Mark

Ch21, Iceberg photograph by Andreas Weith courtesy of Wikimedia Commons, under Creative Commons Attribution-Share Alike 4.0 International, https://creativecommons.org/licenses/by-sa/4.0/deed.en

Ch27, *Wreckers – Coast of Northumberland, with a Steam-Boat Assisting a Ship off Shore* by J.M.W. Turner, courtesy of the Yale Center for British Art, New Haven, Connecticut, USA, https://britishart.yale.edu (accession no. B1978.43.15)

Ch28, Grace Darling rowing out to sea in a furious storm. Colour wood engraving by E. Evans after C.J. Staniland, courtesy of the Wellcome

Collection, https://wellcomecollection.org designated Creative Commons, Public Domain Mark

Ch30, © Parks Canada, 14 Sept 2021, with kind permission

Ch34, Image of pocketwatch, courtesy of the Council of the National Army Museum, London

Ch34, Great white shark underwater, Fiona Ayerst/Shutterstock.com [stock photo ID 1871947789]

Ch37, Demonstration of breeches buoy, courtesy of Library of Congress Prints and Photographs Division, Washington DC, 20540, USA; Star Lifebuoys by Michael Elleray, https://www.flickr.com/photos/mike_elleray/6821723641/ under Creative Commons Attribution 2.0 Generic (CC BY 2.0) https://creativecommons.org/licenses/by/2.0/

Ch38, photograph of James Russell, courtesy of State Library Victoria, https://www.slv.vic.gov.au

Ch39, Wreck chart for 1859, courtesy of the Wellcome Collection, https://wellcomecollection.org designated Creative Commons, Public Domain Mark

Ch46, photograph of *Cospatrick*, courtesy of State Library Victoria, https://www.slv.vic.gov.au

Ch50, Captain Clark's trunk, courtesy of John Burland

Ch52, deep sea sonar image of wrecked ship's remains, © Australian Transport Safety Bureau with kind permission

Ch56, image of *Drummond Castle* chalice, by Gzen92, [File:Église Saint-Ronan – calice Drummond Castle (Île-Molène).jpg] courtesy of Wikimedia Commons, under Creative Commons Attribution-Share Alike 4.0 International license, https://creativecommons.org/licenses/by-sa/4.0/deed.en

Ch58, Liverpool Cathedral staircase window, Mary Rogers; photograph © David Dixon, https://creativecommons.org/licenses/by-sa/2.0/ accessed via https://www.geograph.org.uk/

Ch59, Marconi operator aboard ship *Deutschland* at his instruments; courtesy of Library of Congress Prints and Photographs Division, Washington DC, 20540, USA

Ch64, Captain A.H. Rostron & Mrs J.J. Brown; George Grantham Bain Collection, courtesy of Library of Congress Prints and Photographs Division, Washington DC, 20540, USA

Ch65, The burning *Volturno*; courtesy of Library of Congress Prints and Photographs Division, Washington DC, 20540, USA

Ch66, Dr James F. Grant, ship's surgeon, fixing up Gordon C. Davidson; George Grantham Bain Collection, courtesy of Library of Congress Prints and Photographs Division, Washington DC, 20540, USA

Ch71, London opinion 'Your country needs you'/ Alfred Leete; courtesy of Library of Congress Prints and Photographs Division, Washington DC, 20540, USA

Ch73, *Glenart* Castle memorial by Etchacan1974 courtesy of Wikimedia Commons, under Creative Commons Attribution-Share Alike

Ch75, Aerial photograph showing the aftermath of the Zeebrugge Raid, HMSO

Ch79, Only and exclusive photo of *Vestris* as it went down (Fred Hanson) J 299784 US Copyright Office; Remarkable photo of the *Vestris* disaster (Fred Hanson) J 299787 US Copyright Office. Both courtesy of Library of Congress Prints and Photographs Division, Washington DC, 20540, USA

Ch95, MV *Derbyshire* Memorial 2 by Rodhullandemu courtesy of Wikimedia Commons, under Creative Commons Attribution-Share Alike 4.0 International,

Ch96, Sea Lion Island, Falkland Islands – c.2017: memorial to those lost on HMS *Sheffield* during the Falklands War, Al Clark /Shutterstock.com [stock photo ID 1442824847]

Introduction

I am the first generation of my father's family since Elizabethan times not to go to sea in one capacity or another: fisherman, merchant service or Royal Navy. However, unsurprisingly, I have inherited a love of the sea, as well as a respect for it – not least because my family has had a long association with wrecked ships. In 1779 my forebear Thomas Wills was aboard HMS *Arethusa* when it was wrecked off the coast of Brittany. The details of this story survived in my family for generations and the tale is told in chapter 16.

Many of my kin were officers or seamen on merchant ships in the nineteenth century, when it was a dangerous time to be afloat. For example,

Captain Richard Wills's vessel *The Fly* was lost, taking him with it, in 1800, and Captain Thomas Wills and his ship left port in 1842 and were never seen again. As if bereavement were not bad enough for the wives and children of these men, in most cases the loss of the main breadwinner plunged them into poverty.

My great-grandfather, another Richard, was coxswain of the Poole lifeboat and during his career he saved the lives of 120 people from shipwreck. Remarkably, this included rescuing the crew of a Japanese submarine in 1919. On another occasion he was confronted by a French captain carrying a revolver while on the deck of a ship in distress: despite the danger to the

Richard Wills the lifeboat coxswain (seated centre) with his crew.

vessel, the captain did not want his ship claimed as salvage.

Finally, my grandfather served with a naval patrol ship off the west coast of Scotland in the First World War. They reported U-boat sightings and made weather reports, but were also tasked to keep a look-out for lifeboats and life-rafts carrying shipwreck survivors. On one occasion they came across a boat overloaded with seamen who had abandoned ship but all had died of thirst or exposure. 'No-one wants to know their son or husband died like this,' said the commander. 'Sink it. No entry in the log.'

Having all these family connections, it is not surprising that I have chosen a career that involves researching, writing and talking on the subject of historical shipwrecks. It's a topic that I am often asked to advise about. For example, I appeared as an expert in the episode of BBC's

Who Do You Think You Are? devoted to the singer Cheryl. Her forebear, like one of mine, simply disappeared along with his ship and crew in 1858. Although not included in the TV programme, an ancestor of former politician and broadcaster Ed Balls was wrecked in the fog on HMS *Skylark* in 1845 but was rescued. Actor Liz Carr's grandfather's ship narrowly missed a U-boat's torpedo in the First World War, and Liz remarked that if the torpedo had hit, then she probably wouldn't be here. So shipwrecks have the potential to significantly change the course of history.

A good example of this is the *White Ship*, which sank in 1120. The foundering of this vessel changed the course of history since the only legitimate heir of King Henry I died in the incident. The loss of his son plunged the king into grief and, on his death, England suffered

An image of every British ship lost in 1905.

eighteen years of devastating civil war while the rival claimants to the throne slugged it out across the kingdom.

I had originally intended to feature the *White Ship* as a chapter in this book. However, after some consideration, I decided to begin my narrative in the sixteenth century. This is mainly because there are scant details concerning most wrecks that happened before then, the *White Ship* being a notable exception.

After finalising my era of interest, my next biggest difficulty was determining which subjects to write about. I decided from the outset that this was not to be a book about 'the 100 worst shipwrecks'. The story of ships lost at sea is, of course, often the story of those who died, but it is also the story of heroic rescues, incredible survivals and the improvements in safety that ultimately have made deaths at sea much less likely.

Inevitably, confining myself to one hundred objects over the period of half a millennium means that a huge number of potential topics cannot be included. Shipwrecks were depressingly common in the past, so I could easily have written a book about the history of shipwrecks focusing on just a single year. In 1906, for example, the *Illustrated London News* commissioned a pictorial representation of every British shipwreck from the previous year. It featured 623 vessels lost throughout the British Empire.

When deciding whether to include a subject, I have tended to be guided by two factors. First, is there a notable personal story to tell? History is much more interesting, in my mind, when it can be related to the actions or experiences of an individual because we can attempt to put ourselves in their place. The second factor that helped me to decide whether to include a subject was whether it contributed something to the overall narrative of our ancestors' experiences

at sea across the centuries. This over-arching story builds across the book as a whole and it has led me to omit shipwrecks that were similar to others already included, even if they are well known. I have also tried to include wrecks of British ships from all around the world: Europe, Australia, Asia, North and South America, even a Polar wreck.

I hope you think that I have made good decisions about what to include.

A Note About Figures for Survivors and Victims

For many wrecks, other than comparatively recent ones, it is impossible to be precise about the number of people who died or survived. There are many reasons for this. Contemporary sources such as ship-owners' records, official inquiries, passenger and crew lists, and newspapers often disagree about the figures. In the case of SS *London* (chapter 40), there were crewmembers who joined at the last minute and so were not documented on the official crew list, a number of unidentified stowaways, and people who were considered too unimportant to enumerate, such as the servants of first class passengers. The crew of SS *Jeddah* (chapter 50) confessed that they did not bother to count children when they drew up their passenger list. Sometimes there was no legal requirement to keep a list of passengers – in the case of the river ferry *Princess Alice* (chapter 49), the coroner admitted that his figure of around 650 victims was simply an estimate because there was no way to know the true total.

Even on military vessels, where records are often more complete and reliable, there can be confusion. Crew joined and left at the last minute, and ships might carry non-enumerated individuals for all sorts of reasons. When HMS *Royal George* sank in harbour in 1782 (chapter 17), there were unknown numbers of visitors, family members, victuallers and repairers on board. Intriguingly, DNA analysis of some of the remains of people who died subsequent to the sinking of HMS *Terror* and HMS *Erebus* (chapter 30) suggests there may have been unidentified women on board. These might have been wives, unofficial sick berth assistants or even sex workers. This seems to have been quite common in the Royal Navy before the later nineteenth century.

Differing figures have been quoted historically for the number of casualties arising from the loss of HMS *Hood* in 1941. The initial Admiralty figure of around 1,425 was later altered when some 'victims' turned out not to have been on board due to desertion or illness. One man who had died on another ship had also been included by mistake. It was not until the 1980s that the true figure of 1,415 deaths was finalised following careful research.

For all these reasons, I have often given the numbers of survivors and victims as approximations, sometimes quoting a middling figure where there is an unresolvable disparity.

1

Sea monster depiction

Monsters of the deep were believed to be responsible for wrecking ships

Our medieval and Tudor ancestors were suspicious of the deep oceans and of venturing too far from the protection of land. Seafarers were familiar with whales, but what other huge beasts might lie in wait beneath the surface ready to apprehend and wreck a luckless ship? The sea serpent Leviathan was mentioned in the Bible so people believed that such creatures really existed. Fear of the unknown, vivid imaginations and distorted representations of real creatures led to accounts of monstrous beasts that would supposedly attack an unfortunate crew and destroy their ship. These perils of the deep surely explained why some vessels never arrived at their expected destination. In many ways, perhaps, monsters were the personifications of people's anxieties about ocean travel.

Conrad Gessner was a Swiss naturalist, who in 1551 published the first volume of his masterwork *Historia Animalium*. It was written in Latin, the universal language of the educated European, and was popular in Britain. Gessner did something that no one had attempted before: he described and depicted every known animal. Although he included his own personal observations, he could not see all the animals himself, and for these species he relied on sources such as ancient classical writers, as well as contemporary European scholars. The theme for Gessner's volume four was fishes, and here he included the sea serpent illustrated below. He copied this image from an illustration by Swedish cartographer Olaus Magnus, printed in 1539.

Written accounts of historical sea monsters by British seafarers are rare. However, on his return

from Newfoundland in 1583, Sir Humphrey Gilbert claims to have seen a strange creature:

> There passed along between us and towards the land which we now forsook a very lion to our seeming, in shape, hair, and colour, not swimming after the manner of a beast by moving of his feet, but rather sliding upon the water with his whole body, excepting the legs, in sight . . . Thus he passed along turning his head to and fro, yawing and gaping wide, with ugly demonstration of long teeth, and glaring eyes; and to bid us a farewell, coming right against the hind [=stern], he sent forth a horrible voice, roaring or bellowing as doth a lion . . .

In August 1848 the crew of HMS *Daedalus* reported sighting a sea serpent between the island of St Helena and the Cape of Good Hope. It was shaped like a giant snake at least 60 feet long, its jaws were full of large jagged teeth, and its mouth seemed 'sufficiently capacious to admit of a tall man standing upright'. The ship's company watched the beast for twenty minutes, and the captain later prepared a report for the Admiralty and was interviewed about it in *The Times*. The crew's description remains a mystery.

A sketch of the sea serpent seen in 1848 from HMS *Daedalus*.

2

Rosary from Mary Rose

Henry VIII's favourite warship sank in front of him in 1545

This rosary was one of many found amongst the remains of *Mary Rose*. One can imagine a despairing crewmember clutching at these Christian prayer beads to seek divine protection or comfort as the ship sank beneath him.

Mary Rose was a small ship by modern standards – just 600 tons – and it was ordered to be built in Portsmouth by royal command in 1510. The ship had a successful military career, being widely praised for its sailing ability.

In July 1545 a large French fleet sailed into the Solent. The smaller English fleet was ready for them, and Henry VIII took up a position on Southsea Castle to observe the encounter. The French were using galleys powered by rowers so initially had an advantage because there was no wind, but a breeze picked up, enabling the English ships to engage the enemy.

Mary Rose fired her starboard guns, then came about to fire from the port side. Unfortunately, the starboard gun ports were not closed before this manoeuvre and there was a sudden gust of wind as the vessel turned. The net effect was that *Mary Rose* was seen to heel over with the wind, apparently pushing the open gun ports below water. The sea gushed in, flooding the lower deck and dragging the ship down so that it sank in

only a few minutes. In this era few people could swim and nearly everyone on board drowned, including Sir George Carew, who was newly in command of the ship. There were about five hundred men serving on *Mary Rose* and only thirty-five or so survived.

The ship had recently been refitted and extra guns added, which may have affected the vessel's stability and been at least partly to blame for its foundering. The French also claimed to have fired on the ship and sunk it: a cannonball striking at or below the water line might have initiated or exacerbated the influx of water that was to prove so fatal. The precise reasons for the sinking will probably never be known.

One can only imagine the king's reaction to watching the loss of his most prestigious warship so early in the engagement. However, the battle was not lost. Neither fleet managed to secure an advantage over the other, and after four days the French retreated.

Almost immediately the English set about trying to salvage *Mary Rose*, employing Venetian experts to raise the ship, but they were unsuccessful. The wreck was rediscovered in 1836 and plundered by salvagers for collectables, but was then forgotten. In the late 1960s the remains were located once more and in 1982 the hull was raised from the seabed using a specially constructed frame, and it is now on display at Portsmouth's Historic Dockyard.

Apart from preserving an invaluable part of the UK's heritage, the saving of *Mary Rose* led to the introduction of the Protection of Wrecks Act so that future wrecksites might be safeguarded for their historical, archaeological or artistic value.

The remains of the hull and decks of *Mary Rose*.

3

Armada medal

Issued to mark the defeat of the Spanish Armada by the English, but the weather claimed many ships

In July 1588 England was bracing itself for invasion. King Philip II of Spain had sent a mighty armada of 130 ships that were to pick up troops and land them in England. However, what began as an attempt to conquer an infuriating Protestant nation ended with dismal failure and the dispersal and wrecking of multiple Spanish ships. England was saved by the plucky resistance and skill of its navy under Lord Howard of Effingham, assisted by Sir Francis Drake and Sir John Hawkins, but also by the fortuitous intervention of

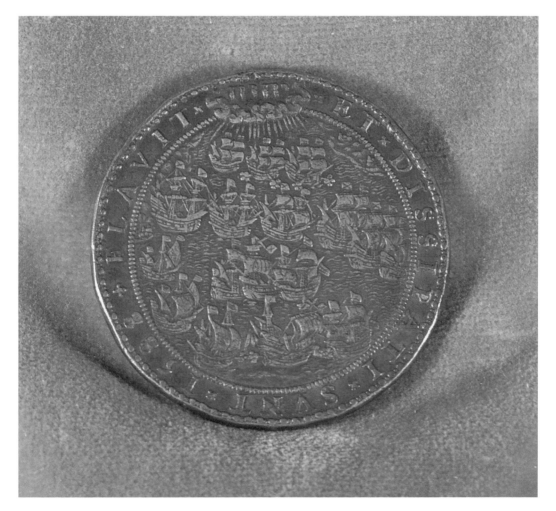

the weather. The armada medal depicts the English chasing damaged Spanish ships, and was minted by England's Protestant allies, the Dutch. Its legend acknowledges the role of the wind in achieving victory: 'Jehovah blew and they were scattered.'

Shortly after the armada first entered the English Channel, two ships were abandoned after colliding with each other. Later, five more were lost off Dunkirk, where the frustrated Spanish were unable to embark their soldiers needed for the invasion. Harassed constantly by the English navy and the Dutch, and powerless to complete the mission as planned, the Spaniards made the fateful decision to return to Spain. With their direct route home via the Channel blocked by the English, the armada sailed into the North Sea and attempted to round Scotland and Ireland. They were chased by the English about as far as the Firth of Forth to prevent them coming ashore.

The Spanish were totally unfamiliar with these northern waters, and severe storms arose off the coast of Scotland and Ireland that made matters worse. Some ships had been badly damaged by English cannon-fire, but the wind and waves ripped away masts, sails and rigging. Ship after ship was wrecked. In Scotland *El Gran Grifón*, one of the flagships, was driven ashore at Fair Isle, whilst *San Juan de Sicilia* mysteriously blew up while refitting at Tobermory, perhaps due to the action of English agents.

However, the Irish coast was to claim more than twenty victims, including *La Trinidad Valencera* (Kinnagoe Bay, Donegal), *La Juliana*, *Lavia* and *Santa María de Visón* (Streedagh, County Sligo), *Santa Maria de La Rosa* (Blasket Sound, County Kerry), *San Esteban* (Doonbeg, County Clare), and *Girona* (Antrim). Some Spaniards stumbling ashore were secretly welcomed into Irish Catholic communities, but many were killed and their bodies and ships plundered. At least one vessel, *Santiago*, was wrecked as far away as Norway.

By the time the remnants of the armada reached a Spanish port, the once-great fleet had lost around half its ships and as many as three-quarters of its personnel. The mighty King of Spain had been rebuffed. England was a small nation that felt it had been protected by God against the Catholic superpower that was Spain, courtesy of a 'Protestant wind'. This is a potent example of how shipwrecks have shaped history.

4

Coat of arms of Bermuda

An island nation with origins in an English shipwreck from 1609

Bermuda comprises a group of islands in the north Atlantic. Its coat of arms has two notable features: a red lion, representing Britain, and a ship striking rocks amidst the waves of a furious storm.

The ship portrayed is *Sea Venture*, which left Plymouth with six other ships in 1609, laden with settlers and supplies for the struggling British settlement of Jamestown, Virginia. It never arrived.

On 24 July 1609 the fleet encountered powerful storms. One ship foundered and the remainder became separated. *Sea Venture* struggled against the wind and waves, leaking so badly that the crew and passengers had to work the pumps and bail out around the clock. Some of the cargo and even the ship's guns were heaved overboard. As the crew became exhausted, the water in the hold reached critical levels, so that sinking was imminent. Yet by good fortune, land was sighted on the morning of 25 July. It was decided to run the ship aground in order to save lives, and as a result *Sea Venture* was sailed onto the rocky shore of Bermuda.

These islands were already known but uninhabited. Their isolated position, tempestuous coasts and the strange calls of wildlife had lent them a sinister name: the Isle of Devils. According to one contemporary account, Bermuda was populated by wicked spirits, and was 'feared and avoided of all sea travellers alive, above any other place in the world'.

One hundred and fifty people survived the wrecked *Sea Venture*, including Sir George Somers, the admiral of the Virginia Company of London that had sent forth the fleet. Together they were stranded on Bermuda for nine months.

They were well-provisioned from the ship's stores and the edible bounty of the island, but there were many setbacks. There were deaths, even a murder, and multiple rebellions which were put down mercifully until in the end one ring-leader was court-martialled and shot. Remarkably, the survivors built two new ships: the appropriately named *Deliverance* and *Patience*. They used wood and rigging salvaged from the wreck of *Sea Venture* as well as locally sourced timber. By May 1610 the ships were ready to sail and departed for Jamestown, arriving safely. Two seamen named Carter and Waters were left behind in Bermuda: the islands' first permanent settlers. The colony began to expand when given its first governor in 1612.

Sir George Somers returned to the islands in late 1610 to collect further supplies for Jamestown but died there. His body was taken back to England, yet for centuries the islands were popularly known as the Somers Isles in his honour.

Accounts by two of the castaways stranded on Bermuda were published shortly after their return to England and are believed to have inspired one of the last of Shakespeare's plays, *The Tempest*.

5

Cannon from Trial

A shipwreck which led to the first English people setting foot in Australia in 1622

*T**rial* belonged to the East India Company, and set sail to Indonesia on 4 September 1621 under the command of John Brookes, with a crew of about 140. Although traders, Company ships had to be heavily armed with guns to resist attacks from pirates and rival European trading nations. This well-preserved cannon was salvaged from *Trial*'s wreck in 1985, although the wooden gun carriage is a reproduction.

Trial's voyage was a lengthy one at a time when a significant proportion of the globe was uncharted, indeed unknown, so maps were primitive. To put this into historical perspective, *Trial* departed England only two years after *Mayflower* carried the Pilgrim Fathers to the fledgling colony of America, and Australia was still largely unmapped and would not be settled by the British until the First Fleet arrived in 1788.

The Suez Canal did not exist in 1621, so ships sailed around the southerly tip of Africa and then crossed the Indian Ocean towards Indonesia. None of Brookes' crew had ever taken this route, and at the Cape of Good Hope he tried to persuade more experienced sailors to join them, but in vain. They departed Africa in March, but at about 11pm on 25 May 1622 *Trial* struck a reef. Captain Brookes, his son and nine others grabbed a small boat called a skiff, while the Company's agent, Thomas Bright, and thirty-five men boarded the longboat. *Trial* broke up and over ninety men were left to drown.

Bright later claimed that, after reassuring him otherwise, the captain abandoned ship secretly: escaping down a rope and leaving everyone else to their fate. Bright maintained that while the ship was sinking the captain loaded the skiff with personal possessions and stole valuables from the cargo. This may or may not be true, but is consistent with the personality of Captain Brookes, who was both devious and dishonest. For example, he later falsified *Trial*'s

position when he reported to the East India Company so that he could blame the wreck on inaccurate nautical charts rather than his own poor navigation.

Both boats carrying survivors eventually reached Indonesia, separately. However, on their journey of some 1,800 miles, the thirty-six men in Bright's longboat stopped at the Monte Bello islands, Western Australia, for a week. These were the first English people ever to stand on Australian soil.

Back in England, Brookes made his excuses to the East India Company about the unreliability of maritime charts and was exonerated. However, they came to regret not investigating the matter more thoroughly, and particularly their decision to re-employ Brookes. In 1625 he was in command of *Moone*, which was also lost. Brookes was suspected of wrecking the ship deliberately and of stealing valuable cargo, and was imprisoned. Yet when the matter was brought to a head, he showed considerable guile and was acquitted again. This time the Company did not re-employ him.

Hull timbers of Sparrow-Hawk

Remains of an English ship carrying colonists to Virginia, wrecked at Massachusetts in 1626

The frame of this ship was revealed by a storm in 1863, recovered, reassembled and exhibited in public. These are the only extant timbers of a seventeenth-century English vessel that crossed the Atlantic. The remains of the hull illustrate the small size of vessels that could be used for oceanic travel at this time: it is estimated that *Sparrow-Hawk* was only about 40 feet long.

According to an account by William Bradford, the governor of Plymouth, Massachusetts, the ship had been bound for Virginia with settlers. After six weeks afloat they had exhausted their supply of water and the captain was so ill with scurvy that he could not leave his cabin. They were lost and feared death by starvation or disease, so decided to run for the nearest shore. By chance they made Cape Cod, but in stormy

seas were washed over a sand-bar into a shallow harbour where at low tide they unloaded the ship to save their possessions. *Sparrow-Hawk* was damaged but repairable if wood could be found.

Some native Americans in canoes came to investigate the shipwreck victims and, much to their surprise, addressed them in English. They agreed to convey two of the crew to William Bradford, together with a letter requesting food and materials to repair the ship. Bradford duly obliged, supplying all their needs, and came back with the native men himself to meet the crew and passengers of *Sparrow-Hawk*.

Not long after his return to Plymouth, Bradford received a message that the newly restored *Sparrow-Hawk* had been blown ashore during a storm and wrecked a second time. This time the damage was beyond repair. The settlers appealed to Bradford to allow them to live with his citizens at Plymouth until they could move on to Virginia. Bradford agreed. He had come to Massachusetts with the Pilgrim Fathers on *Mayflower* in 1620 and must have felt a kinship for these brave colonists.

Unfortunately, some of the fresh arrivals at Plymouth soon offended this devoutly Christian community. Notably, one Mr Fells kept a female servant as a concubine. He denied it robustly, but a few months later she fell pregnant and they tried to run away. There were others who exhibited behaviour which Bradford describes tactfully as 'untoward'. Whatever the issues, the Plymouth colony was keen to get rid of their new friends as soon as they could, and in summer the following year they were packed off to Virginia on two ships. It all seems to have ended amicably, however, Bradford noting that 'sundrie of them have acknowledged their thankfullnes since, from Virginia'.

Meanwhile the wreck of *Sparrow-Hawk* was buried by sand on a coastline where sediments move about rapidly, ensuring its remarkable preservation.

Pocket sundial from the warship
London

Recovered 350 years after this naval vessel blew up in the Thames estuary in 1665

London was built by order of Oliver Cromwell in 1656, yet ironically was part of the convoy that conducted Charles II back to England from exile in 1660. This ship was a notable vessel in the Restoration navy and its sudden destruction by accident in March 1665 caused national shock. Diarist Samuel Pepys described the breaking news:

> This morning is brought me to the office the sad newes of "The London," in which [Vice-admiral] Sir J. Lawson's men were all

bringing her from Chatham to the Hope [near Tilbury], and thence he was to go to sea in her; but a little a'this side the buoy of the Nower [near Sheerness], she suddenly blew up. About 24 [men] and a woman that were in the round-house and coach [were] saved; the rest, being above 300, drowned: the ship breaking all in pieces, with 80 pieces of brass ordnance. She lies sunk, with her round-house above water. Sir J. Lawson hath a great loss in this of so many good chosen men, and many relations among them. I went to the 'Change [Royal Exchange], where the news taken very much to heart. So home to dinner . . .

Diarist and physician John Evelyn was one of the commissioners responsible for medical support to the navy, and wrote: 'I went to receive the poor creatures that were saved out of the *London* frigate, blown up by accident, with above 200 men.'

The precise cause of the ship's violent destruction is not known. However, the explosion was sudden and forceful – sufficient to destroy the ship beyond any hope of salvage. England had just commenced the Second Anglo-Dutch War, but no suspicion of enemy sabotage was voiced at the time; the ship was also not reported as catching fire beforehand.

The only realistic mechanism for such a catastrophe is accidental ignition of the vessel's stores of gunpowder. Ammunition was kept below the waterline in a restricted area known as the ship's magazine, where naked flames were forbidden. One can only suppose that this rule was breached in some way. Many sailors smoked tobacco, and candle lanterns were the only method of lighting available so, almost inevitably, fires and explosions at sea did happen.

The exquisite pocket sundial was retrieved from the mud of the Thames estuary, and is a little over 5cm wide. It is so well preserved that the digits around its circumference are distinct and it still retains its glass components. It clearly belonged to a person of means, and may even have been in the pocket of an officer at the time of the tragedy. It is one of a number of significant twenty-first-century finds from the wreck including cannon, a shoe, spoons, bottles and tiles, pulley blocks, barrels, a comb, a surgeon's syringe, and even portions of ship's rope and beeswax candles. The true death toll will never be known but was likely to have exceeded 300 people.

North Foreland lighthouse

A seventeenth-century lighthouse, one of many that helped prevent shipwrecks

The story of shipwrecks is as much about attempts to prevent them as the shipwrecks themselves. Cliff-top lights on the Isle of Thanet have warned sailors about the nearby Goodwin Sands since 1499, but a proper lighthouse was not built until 1636. Unfortunately, it was made of wood and burned down, but was replaced by the current North Foreland lighthouse in 1691. The new structure was 'a strong house of flint, an octagon, on the top of which was an iron grate quite open to the air, in which was made a blazing fire of coals'.

Lighthouses are not a recent invention. They were used by the ancient Greeks and Romans; perhaps most famously the Pharos Lighthouse of Alexandria, Egypt, was one of the Seven Wonders of the Ancient World. A second-century Roman lighthouse stands in the grounds of Dover Castle, 20 miles from the North Foreland lighthouse. It is one of only three still standing anywhere in the world.

For centuries lighthouses were only built on land because it was technically impossible to construct them offshore. This meant that locations with submerged rocks were notoriously hazardous to shipping, such as Bell Rock (Angus), Eddystone (Cornwall) and Penmon Point (Anglesey).

In 1698 Henry Winstanley completed the first ever offshore lighthouse at Eddystone. It was wooden and was swept away along with its creator by the Great Storm of 1703. A wooden replacement lasted longer, but burned down in 1755. A major step forward came when John Smeaton designed a more stable shape for a lighthouse based on an oak tree, having a broad base that swept up into a tower. His creation at Eddystone was made of stone, and Smeaton also pioneered the use of hydraulic lime, a concrete that set under water. Smeaton's work inspired the building of lighthouses in other dangerous offshore areas.

Lighthouses needed to evolve to burn substances other than coal. In 1698 the North Foreland lighthouse consumed 100 tons of coal annually: this was expensive, cumbersome and inefficient. In the 1730s the owners experimented with covering the top of the lighthouse, using bellows to keep the fire going, and broadcasting the light through windows. This reduced fuel costs and prevented the beacon being extinguished by rain or wind, but the light was too weak and the number of local wrecks escalated.

By the nineteenth century, lighthouses burned oil rather than coal, and used lenses and mirrors to magnify the light produced so that it could be seen from much further away. The final evolution of lighthouses was for them to operate automatically, abolishing the lonely role of lighthouse-keeper. In 1922 the Penmon Point lighthouse was the first to be automated, whereas North Foreland was the last to lose its keeper, converting to full automation in 1998.

Penmon Point lighthouse (Trwyn Du) at Beaumaris, Anglesey, in the fog.

Giant clam collected by William Dampier

A buccaneer, cartographer, explorer and collector wrecked in the Atlantic in 1701

William Dampier was born in 1651. As the son of a farmer, there was no expectation that he would pursue a maritime career. Nevertheless, at 17 he went to sea and subsequently joined the navy, fighting in the Anglo-Dutch War. After military service, he worked on a Caribbean plantation, then became a privateer and even a pirate, travelling as far as Australia, then known as New Holland. He published a selective account of his adventures, which was an immediate success.

The Admiralty realised that Dampier could be an asset because few Englishmen had visited New Holland and little of it had been

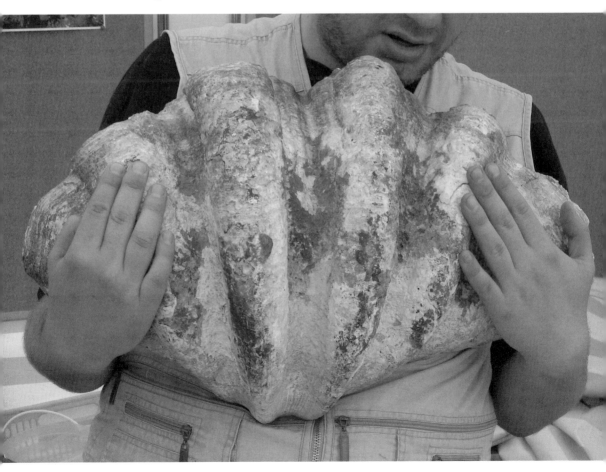

charted. So, despite his shady past, Dampier was commissioned to map its coast. He was not a trained naval officer and yet he was given command of HMS *Roebuck* and set sail in 1698.

Dampier clashed repeatedly with the ship's second in command, Lieutenant George Fisher, who probably resented reporting to a self-confessed buccaneer. Their frequent arguments culminated in Dampier, outrageously, caning the unfortunate Fisher in front of the crew. Quite apart from Fisher's personal humiliation, this was a breathtaking breach of naval protocol since ships' officers were considered gentlemen. Shortly afterwards, Fisher was dumped ashore and *Roebuck* continued without him.

Roebuck reached the dry western coast of Australia in August 1699, where Dampier charted about 870 miles of coastline and collected many natural history specimens. However, with the ship running low on water and many of his men suffering from scurvy, he headed to Timor to replenish their provisions. *Roebuck* was also becoming unseaworthy, so he decided to return to England. There were several stops on the way, but on 21 September 1701, within sight of Ascension Island in the Atlantic, *Roebuck* sprang a serious leak. The carpenter reported that timbers below the waterline were rotten and the ship could not be saved.

Dampier ran the ship aground and ferried as much ashore as he could without losing a single man. They made tents from the ship's sails and managed to subsist for a little over five weeks on turtles and goats, as well as water from a spring. On 3 April four ships were sighted and the castaways were taken home. On arrival, Dampier was court-martialled and found not guilty of causing the loss of *Roebuck* but guilty of abusing Lieutenant Fisher, for which crime he was made to forfeit his entire wages for the voyage.

When the wrecksite of *Roebuck* was found in 2001, the large clam shown on the previous page was recovered, together with the ship's bell. The clam is a species found on the shore of Western Australia and not native to the Atlantic. Dampier had recorded that he collected many shells in Australia, but he lost most of them when *Roebuck* sank at Ascension Island.

The forceful William Dampier.

10

Storm clouds over the sea

Bad weather has wrecked innumerable ships, but the Great Storm of 1703 wreaked havoc

Storms loom large in the history of shipwrecks. They have destroyed countless vessels and probably caused the demise of thousands of ships that simply 'disappeared'. However, the Great Storm of 26 November 1703 was an extreme event that inflicted unprecedented devastation on land and at sea.

Ship losses were extensive because the hurricane was focused on the south of England, the centre for trade and the location of many major ports, as well as the busy English Channel. The Royal Navy lost thirteen ships, including HMS *Restoration*, *Northumberland*, *Stirling Castle* and *Mary*, which were all wrecked on the Goodwin Sands, taking over a thousand men to their deaths. An eyewitness on a nearby warship described the end of HMS *Mary* and the fleet's rear admiral: 'To see Admiral Beaumont, that

33

was next us, and all the rest of his men, how they climbed up the main mast, hundreds at a time crying out for help, and thinking to save their lives, and in the twinkling of an eye were drowned.'

HMS *Newcastle* was lost at Portsmouth and HMS *Reserve* at Yarmouth, with few survivors. Admiral Sir Cloudesley Shovell's ship, HMS *Association*, was blown out of control from Harwich to the coast of Norway, sparking fears that it too had been lost.

Merchant ships were lost, damaged and blown off course in even greater numbers. The author Daniel Defoe explained that no anchor would hold. Even on the Thames in the heart of London the storm savaged around seven hundred ships so that they 'were huddled together and drove on shore, heads and sterns, one upon another, in such a manner, as anyone would have thought it had been impossible: and the damage done on that account was incredible'. Similarly, nearly every one of around eighty ships anchored in

the river Humber near Grimsby were damaged, some sinking, others blown out to sea. Thirty merchant ships from a large convoy sheltering at Milford Haven were destroyed, and three more were missing presumed lost. Defoe calculated that in total at least 150 sailing vessels were lost during the storm.

An especially sad loss was the destruction of the world's first offshore lighthouse at Eddystone, near Plymouth, together with its pioneering designer Henry Winstanley. Yet Defoe concludes his account of the storm with another poignant story. A ship homeward bound from the Caribbean was in imminent danger of foundering, the masts gone and the ship leaking. Filled with despair, the captain called the surgeon and they decided to avoid the unpleasantness of drowning by shooting themselves. The surgeon died immediately but the captain lived just long enough to understand that the ship had been spared and his hasty action had proved unnecessary.

Approaching danger: a storm in the Pacific.

Portrait of Sir Cloudesley Shovell

An illustrious admiral who perished in a notorious naval disaster
at the Isles of Scilly in 1707

Sir Cloudesley Shovell was a man of humble birth who rose to become admiral of the Mediterranean fleet. In October 1707 he was returning from an unsuccessful attempt to capture the French city of Toulon when his twenty-one ships encountered a storm. They were near the western entrance to the English Channel, but the foul weather meant that it was impossible to determine their exact position. Admiral Shovell consulted his senior officers and they determined, by little more than guesswork, that they were near the French island of Ushant and that the way ahead was clear for them to enter the Channel. They were wrong. The fleet was much further north than anticipated. Inexplicably, despite his decades of experience, the admiral decided to sail north-eastwards into the Channel at night, in a rainy gale, and without being certain where he was.

Tragically, Shovell led his fleet right onto rocks off the Scilly Isles. The admiral's mighty flagship, HMS *Association*, struck first and went down immediately with all hands. It had a crew of about eight hundred as well as many passengers. *Association* was followed by *Eagle*, which met the same fate, and then the smaller *Romney*. Several other ships escaped destruction only by the narrowest of margins. HMS *Firebrand* was a small vessel and was lifted clear after striking so that about twenty-three of its crew were spared. The only other survivor was George Lawrence, *Romney*'s quartermaster. HMS *Phoenix* was so badly damaged that it was run ashore to save the ship; fortunately no one was killed.

The total number who died is not known for certain but it may have been nearly two thousand men. The admiral's body was amongst the first to be found washed ashore. He had been stripped of valuables, including two rings, one of which held a large emerald set with diamonds. Enquiries were set in place to try to locate this valuable item, but came to nothing. Meanwhile Admiral Shovell's corpse was embalmed and transported to London, and he received a lavish state funeral in Westminster Abbey at Queen Anne's expense.

And that might have been the end of this sad story, except that about twenty-five years later a clergyman on the Scilly Isles is said to have attended the deathbed confession of a local woman. She told him that Admiral Shovell had been cast ashore exhausted and faint but still living, and that she had murdered him for the sake of his valuables. She produced the ring, explaining that she had been afraid to sell such a well-known jewel in case it led to her discovery, and asked that it be returned. It was given to the admiral's close friend, the Earl of Berkeley.

Sr. CLOUDISLLY SHOVELL KNIGHT, Rear Admiral of the
Red on Board their Ma.ties Ship the Royal William in yᵉ
late defeat given to the French, and also Lieut. Colᴸ. of one of
their Maᵗⁱᵉˢ Marine Regiments.

W. De Ryck pinx: I. Smith fec:

12

Pirate flag 'Jolly Roger'

Flown by many pirates, but they were responsible for comparatively few shipwrecks

This modern reproduction of a pirate flag carries some features described as being used by British pirates in the early eighteenth century, although no examples survive from the period. Different pirates had different versions, but their flags often featured various assortments of white bones or skulls on a black background. Pirates might fly any number of national flags to try to disguise their true identity. The 'Jolly Roger' was traditionally only hoisted when they were within firing range of a target to indicate their real intentions.

Generally, it was not in a pirate's best interest to wreck or destroy their prey. It was preferable for a merchant ship to surrender without a fight,

in the hope that the pirates would plunder the cargo but spare the ship and the lives of those on board. However, some pirates did wreck others' ships. For example, in 1720 John 'Black Bart' Roberts sailed into Trepassey in Newfoundland with 'black colours flying, drums beating, and trumpets sounding'. The mere sight of his Jolly Roger caused the men on twenty-two ships in the harbour to flee. When Black Bart left, he kept one of the ships but set fire to all the rest.

In many respects, pirates became better known for destroying their own ships than other people's. A pirate's ship had to be robust, speedy, well-armed and big enough to house not just all the booty but a comparatively large

crew as well as the stores needed to sustain them. Their vessels often saw damaging action, and the warm waters of the Caribbean were not friendly to wooden hulls, so pirate captains frequently acquired new ships, destroying their previous flagship when it seemed to be falling short of the mark.

Yet not all pirate ship losses were intentional. In April 1717 the notorious 'Black Sam' Bellamy was at sea off Cape Cod, Massachusetts, when his ship *Whydah* was caught in a violent storm and forced onto the shoals, capsized and burst apart. The next day the bodies of around one hundred pirates were washed ashore. The remains of *Whydah* were rediscovered by divers in 1984. Subsequent excavation has recovered the ship's bell bearing its name, as well as a cannon, precious stones, gold and more than fifteen thousand coins.

Another wrecked pirate ship to have been rediscovered is believed to be the flagship of perhaps the most famous pirate of all time: Edward Teach, known as 'Blackbeard'. His vessel – the wonderfully named *Queen Anne's Revenge* – ran aground while seeking a sheltered mooring in North Carolina in 1718. Blackbeard escaped the scene unharmed, but the probable remains of his ship were rediscovered in 1996.

Black Bart and his version of the Jolly Roger (printed 1725).

13

First edition of Robinson Crusoe

Daniel Defoe's account of a shipwreck victim, published in 1719, set the standard for the genre

Often described as the earliest English novel in a modern style, the first edition of this book does not bear Daniel Defoe's name. Instead, it is portrayed as being the autobiography of a genuine shipwreck survivor. The preface even states that the book is a factual account. Its full title is *The Life and Strange Surprizing Adventures of Robinson Crusoe of York, Mariner.* The sense of realism that Defoe evoked in his fictional writing was refreshing and one of the main attractions to his audience; it was an immediate bestseller.

In the book Crusoe is shipwrecked on 30 September 1659 and cast ashore on a small

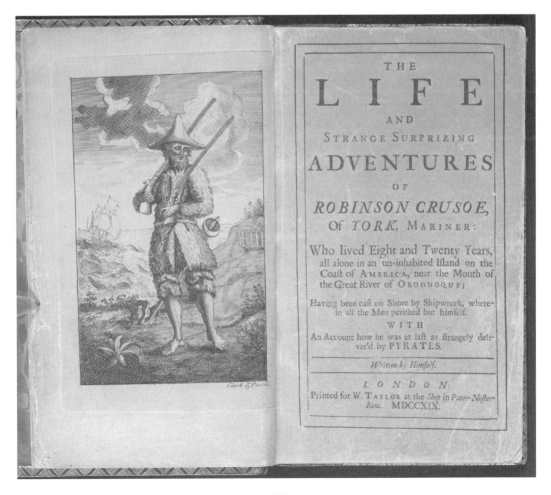

island somewhere in the region of modern Trinidad and Tobago. Of the eleven men on board his ship, Crusoe is the only survivor. He sees none of the others again, but does find three of their hats, one cap and two shoes washed up on the beach. As he studies the distant wreck from the safety of the sands, he is amazed that he made it ashore: 'I cast my eye to the stranded vessel when, the breach and froth of the sea being so big, I could hardly see it, it lay so far off; and considered, Lord! how was it possible I could get on shore?' Much soul-searching, reflection and adventures followed, including Crusoe meeting cannibals, rescuing Man Friday and defeating a group of mutineers so that he can return to England in their ship.

Crusoe is deserted on his 'Island of Despair' for twenty-eight years, and uses great ingenuity to ensure that he survives. Despite the main protagonist's obvious loneliness, there is also an attractive element of escapism that the author evokes well. The novel's enduring success has heavily influenced the popular romanticised perception of being shipwrecked. Not least the image of a man wandering a tropical desert island clad only in animal skins, as depicted opposite the title page of the first edition. The concept of intrepid Europeans surviving against the odds in an alien world after shipwreck inspired many other books, including *Gulliver's Travels*, *Swiss Family Robinson* and the character of Ben Gunn in *Treasure Island*.

Defoe's detailed insights into the life of a castaway were probably informed by multiple non-fictional accounts of being marooned far from home. Scottish sailor Alexander Selkirk, for example, was abandoned for over four years on the Pacific island of Más a Tierra after an argument with his captain. Selkirk was rescued by privateer Woodes Rogers in 1709, who described him as 'a man clothed in goats' skins who looked wilder than the first owners of them'. Más a Tierra was officially renamed Robinson Crusoe Island in 1966.

14

Satellite image of Wager Island, Chile

A remote island named after a notorious eighteenth-century shipwreck

The tale of the loss of HMS *Wager* is an epic worthy of Hollywood. The ship was part of Commodore George Anson's fleet which was to circumnavigate the globe. During appalling weather at Cape Horn in 1741, *Wager*, under Captain David Cheap, became separated from the rest of the fleet. The ship was somewhere off the uncharted coast of Chile in bad weather, heavily damaged; the crew were weakened by scurvy; and Captain Cheap had injured himself in a fall. A brief sighting of land by the carpenter was not believed by the ship's lieutenant, who refused to report it to the captain. It was a fatal error of judgement: that night, 14 May, the ship struck shore. Most men escaped in boats, but several stayed behind where they got drunk and some later drowned.

The crew of *Wager* had landed at a desolate location – later named Wager Island in honour of the infamous events to come. It was the beginning of winter and they had little food or shelter. The gunner, John Bulkeley, and others proposed enlarging the ship's longboat to make a schooner and sailing back round the Horn for Brazil; Captain Cheap wanted to head north to rejoin Anson's fleet. They could not agree, and the eventual result was mutiny. Two things made this outcome almost inevitable. Firstly, within six weeks the one hundred and fifty or so survivors were reduced to a hundred owing to deaths and

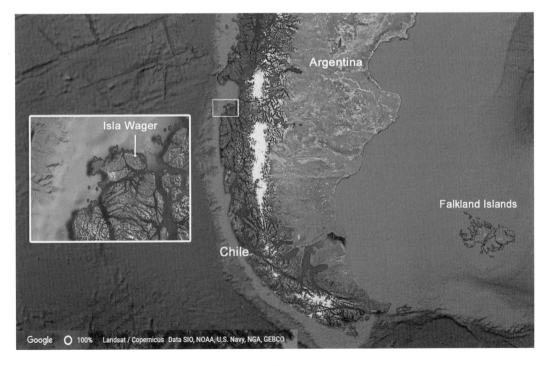

Argentina

Isla Wager

Falkland Islands

Chile

Google   ○ 100%   Landsat / Copernicus Data SIO, NOAA, U.S. Navy, NGA, GEBCO a few desertions. The second factor was Captain Cheap's uncompromising personality: for example, he shot and killed without warning a much-loved midshipman named Henry Cozens.

A complex sequence of events now followed. Bulkeley and the majority departed in the schooner, although two midshipmen returned to Cheap's side when Bulkeley sent back a boat to collect more sails. Both leaders abandoned some of their weakened men, still living, at various points through 'necessity'. Bulkeley's men were freezing, starving and began to die at sea, yet despite all their privations, thirty out of the eighty who left Wager Island reached Rio de Janeiro. They eventually returned to England in 1743.

There were twenty men in Cheap's group, but his attempt to head north failed. Fortunately, after returning to the island, they encountered some local nomads who agreed to lead them overland to a Spanish settlement. Eventually, after lengthy tribulations, Cheap and just three others made it home in 1745. Improbably, three other men abandoned by Bulkeley in Argentina found their way back as well.

The officers at the unavoidable court martial were, perhaps, wise. Mutiny should have attracted a death sentence but the perpetrators had made a miraculous escape against the odds which had captured the public's imagination, and Captain Cheap was both a poor leader and a murderer. They were all acquitted, except for the lieutenant who was reprimanded for not reporting the sighting of land to the captain before the ship wrecked.

The crew used boats to salvage timber and supplies from the wreck of HMS *Wager*.

15

Epic poem The Shipwreck by William Falconer

Written in 1762, these semi-autobiographical verses proved to be a bestseller

Perhaps appropriately, this eighteenth-century copy of William Falconer's *The Shipwreck* holds an antique pressed violet – a symbol of death. Falconer knew all about the tragedy of shipwrecks and the loss of crewmates. As a midshipman, he survived the destruction of the warship *Ramillies* on the coast of Devon in 1760. Due to a miscalculation, the vessel's officers realised too late that they were trapped against the land by an onshore wind. *Ramillies'* anchors would not hold and inexorably it was driven onto the rocks and smashed apart. At the last minute Falconer and twenty-five others bravely leapt for the shore and survived. More than seven hundred others perished. However, this was not Falconer's only brush with death. He was also mate on a merchant ship, *Britannia*, that foundered in the Mediterranean. From the crew of fifty, Falconer was one of only three survivors.

These real-life experiences informed Falconer's greatest poetical work. *The Shipwreck* was

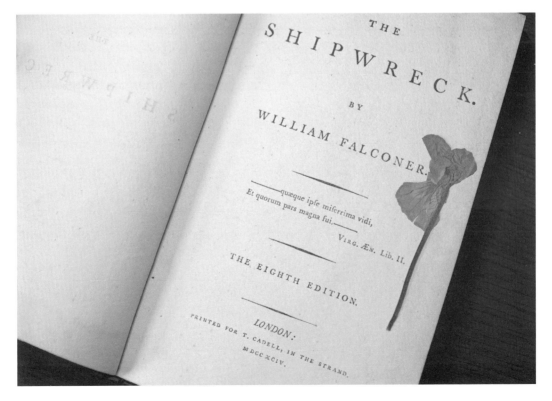

published in 1762 and was an instant success. There were multiple editions in the eighteenth century and it continued to be extremely popular throughout the nineteenth century. The poem runs to over 2,700 lines, and tells the story of the lovers Palemon and Anna, their friend Arion, and the crew of a ship named *Britannia*, on which the two men serve. The vessel is wrecked on the coast of Greece, but they both scramble ashore alive. Yet Arion's joy at finding his friend alive is immediately dashed when he realises Palemon is too badly injured to survive. He dies shortly afterwards, clutching a portrait of his beloved Anna which he had worn around his neck as a pendant. The character of Arion is thought to represent Falconer himself.

Falconer could write about ships and shipwrecks from experience, and he explained nautical terms for lay readers in the form of footnotes. This made it accessible to, and admired by, both seafarers and landsmen alike in an era when deaths at sea were tragically common.

Published success did not oblige Falconer to abandon the sea. By 1769 he had changed services yet again and joined the East India Company. He was purser on *Aurora* in 1769 when its captain unwisely decided to navigate the treacherous Mozambique Channel that runs between the island of Madagascar and mainland Africa. The ship and the ill-fated Falconer were never seen again. A man claiming to be a survivor was interviewed by the ship's owners in 1775; he said that *Aurora* had been wrecked upon rocks. He and four others were the only people to escape.

It seems almost predestined that Falconer, a man who had made his name because of a shipwreck, should eventually die in one. He was just 37 years old.

Arion comforts the dying Palemon in an eighteenth-century illustration from *The Shipwreck*.

16

Château de Fougères

Many crew of HMS Arethusa *were locked in this formidable château when the ship was wrecked*

The ordeal of a shipwreck and its aftermath can linger long in a family's memory. In 1994 my great-uncle told me the story of my ancestor Thomas Wills, whose ship was lost on the Brittany coast. He struggled ashore, only to be imprisoned in a French fortress for a year. The most remarkable thing about this is not that it proved to be true but that it had happened 215 years previously, in 1779. Generations of my family's oral history had preserved the story.

Thomas was coxswain on HMS *Arethusa*. In 1778 it had battled a French frigate, *La Belle Poule*, but did not defeat it. Both ships were badly damaged and drifted apart, yet the French perceived the Royal Navy's failure to capture their frigate as a victory, given Britain's enormous naval superiority. This gained *Arethusa* a certain notoriety on both sides of the Channel.

The following year *Arethusa* chased another French frigate, *L'Aigrette*. After a considerable battering, *L'Aigrette* received reinforcements and

Arethusa backed off. However, later that night the British saw the top-lights of a vessel in the darkness and drifted in to attack. Unfortunately, those lights turned out to be shore lights instead, and *Arethusa* crashed into rocks near Ushant, Brittany. Thomas and his shipmates tried desperately to save their vessel by covering the huge hole with a sail, pumping out seawater and throwing cannon overboard to lighten the ship, but there was no hope. *Arethusa* rapidly filled with water, so they ran it aground just in time and abandoned ship, clawing their way ashore through the rocks and surf where they were soon apprehended by French soldiers. Incredibly, not a single life was lost.

The majority of *Arethusa*'s crew were imprisoned at the impregnable Château de Fougères, about 40 miles south of St Malo. Here they languished under fairly primitive conditions: cramped, with little hygiene and only meagre food rations. The crew were given a small weekly allowance of money and some basic garments since they only had the clothes they had been wrecked in. Family tradition has it that somewhere amidst the maze of the fortress Thomas Wills carved his name into one of the ceiling beams. Perhaps it is still there.

Eventually, after a year of imprisonment, Thomas and some of the other *Arethusa* crew were brought back to England in 1780. There was a prisoner exchange programme with France which meant that captives could effectively be swapped for an equivalent number of enemy men.

The endurance of family stories about shipwreck victims or survivors is almost certainly due to the trauma – or drama – of the events. Yet unfortunately, many of these tales do not conclude as happily as they did for Thomas.

Arethusa battling *La Belle Poule*.

17

Snuff-box made from timbers of HMS Royal George

This ship sank at anchor in broad daylight without storms, fire or enemy action

On 29 August 1782 *Royal George* was moored at Spithead, part of the Solent off Portsmouth. The ship was large, with one hundred guns and a correspondingly sizeable crew. Added to this were workers engaged in maintenance, hundreds of relatives visiting their menfolk, traders selling goods to the crew, victuallers loading stores, and prostitutes. The total number of people on board is not known, but has been estimated at about 1,200.

All of these extra people were permitted on board while the ship was heeled over to one side ('careened'), allowing carpenters to work on parts of the vessel below the waterline. Of course, this made the ship less stable and in

the mid-morning it suddenly began to take on water. One of the carpenters gave a warning of impending danger to a lieutenant, who ignored him, and by the time the captain realised the seriousness of the situation it was too late.

HMS *Royal George* sank like a stone in just a matter of minutes. There are no accurate figures for the total number of lives lost, but the contemporary memorial estimated that about nine hundred people had died, including Rear Admiral Kempenfeldt, who was trapped in his cabin by the influx of water. Around three hundred may have been saved, together with the captain, Martin Waghorn.

At the subsequent court martial Waghorn and other surviving officers were acquitted. It was claimed that a survey of *Royal George* had found some rotten timbers below the waterline, and that the frame of the ship probably broke apart due to the stress of being heeled over. However, it seems more likely that the overloaded ship heeled over too much so that its lower gun ports admitted water. The sloop *Lark* had been loading stores on this lower side too, which added to the warship's instability; *Lark* went down with *Royal George*.

Almost immediately, plans were set in motion to try to recover the wreck, but although some cannon were salvaged, it proved impossible to refloat the ship.

In the 1830s divers recovered more items and found much of the timber still intact. Salvagers raised the oak and it was used to make cheap trinkets of various kinds. This was not considered disrespectful to the dead at the time. The snuff-box show here is typical; it was made in 1839 and bears a gold inscription attesting to its origin. Such was the continued interest in the wreck that an account of the ship's loss and its salvage published in 1840 was popular, and it was actually issued with a cover made from boards of *Royal George* oak. The wood was even used to make billiard tables, although using timbers from an underwater gravesite to construct a game was considered to be in bad taste even by many Victorians. Interestingly, the bronze Corinthian top to Nelson's Column in London was made from *Royal George*'s cannon, which were melted down for the purpose.

Attempting to salvage HMS *Royal George* after its sinking.

18

Bowl and lid from Palau

*A shipwreck that ended happily due to the survivors' ingenuity and their friendship
with Pacific islanders*

*A*ntelope was an East India Company ship, commanded by Henry Wilson. On the night of 10 August 1783 it was in the Pacific, having sailed from Macau in China, when it was beset by a storm. Suddenly, in Captain Wilson's own words: 'the man who was on look-out called *Breakers!*, yet so short was the notice that the call of *Breakers* had scarce reached the officer upon deck before the ship struck'. *Antelope* had run onto a reef belonging to the Palau island group.

It was immediately obvious that their situation was desperate and that the ship could not be repaired: the water was gushing in relentlessly. The crew did everything to preserve their vessel for as long as possible to give them more time to evacuate. Masts were cut away to prevent the ship oversetting, and in a speech the captain begged the crew not to despair or get drunk. The boats were hoisted out and filled with provisions and water, arms and compasses. The crew dressed for abandoning ship, took some refreshment and

then waited until dawn so that they could assess their position.

Daybreak did not bring an end to the storm, but it did allow them to see a small island to which they could row. The crew were fearful that the inhabitants might be hostile, but there seemed to be no one there. The men remaining aboard *Antelope* made a raft to ferry themselves and further provisions and equipment ashore, and when the boats returned they were similarly loaded. Sadly, at this point one man fell overboard and drowned, but miraculously no others were lost, despite the very difficult seas for small boats and the raft. Even the ship's two dogs were saved.

Two days later eight local men appeared in canoes. Despite fears and uncertainties on both sides, a dialogue was established in the Malay language, which one crewmember spoke. Thus began an ongoing warm and friendly relationship between the shipwreck survivors and the local inhabitants' leader, Abba Thulle, who met with them on many occasions.

The castaways decided to use *Antelope*'s timbers to build a new vessel, and were able to retrieve sufficient timber from the wreck for the purpose. Meanwhile, in order to keep good relations, Wilson agreed to requests for some of his men to assist in local battles with Abba Thulle's enemies.

It took three months to construct their ship, *Oroolong*, and in November they departed for Macau, taking with them Abba Thulle's son Lee Boo, at his request, to learn more about European society. From Macau they returned to England. Lee Boo proved an intelligent and charming man who lived with the Wilsons, but sadly he died of smallpox about six months after his arrival.

During one feast with Abba Thulle before their departure, Wilson's group was served a sweet drink from 'a large tureen made of wood in the shape of a bird and inlaid with shell'. This bowl is shown on the previous page, and was one of a number of examples of Palau craftsmanship which were gifted to Wilson and which he brought back with him to England. They are amongst the earliest surviving examples of Palauan objects.

Local leader Abba Thulle.

19

Lifeboat design plans

*Although not honoured in his lifetime, Lionel Lukin designed
the first ever lifeboat in 1785*

Based in London, Lionel Lukin was a coachbuilder with a talent for engineering and original thinking. For example, he invented a rain gauge and a variable reclining bed for use in hospitals. Although not from a seafaring background, when he learned that many lives were lost at sea as a result of boats turning over, Lukin decided to tackle this problem, and his most significant invention was patented in 1785. He called it the 'unimmergible boat' because it would not sink even when filled with water.

Lukin's design incorporated watertight air pockets and cork to increase the buoyancy of the uppermost parts of the boat, but also iron weights at the base (keel) to reduce the risk of the boat capsizing and to assist it to right itself if it did.

His invention came to the attention of John Sharp, Archdeacon of Northumberland, who asked Lukin to convert a local boat to his new design. It was the first ever purpose-built lifeboat and was put into service at Bamburgh, where it saved lives, but the idea was not taken up elsewhere. Lukin shared his designs freely, hoping to inspire others.

However, three years later, in 1789, there was a tragedy. A ship called *Adventure* was wrecked at the mouth of the Tyne, yet in the stormy seas no one could save the crew because local boats were not up to the job. Consequently all the crew drowned. This prompted a local committee to establish a national competition to invent a lifesaving boat that would withstand the violent conditions.

There was no outright winner, but William Wouldhave's metal-hulled design was rated the best and he was offered half the prize money, which offended him greatly. Another entrant, boatbuilder Henry Greathead, was then commissioned to combine features from Wouldhave's design with others, including

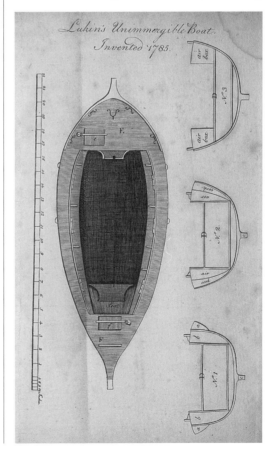

Greathead's own, to build a wooden lifeboat. Although Greathead's boat contained some original features, major aspects were the same as Lukin's, such as the lightweight upper structure and weighted keel.

To Lukin's chagrin, Greathead was lauded as 'the inventor of the lifeboat', granted a substantial monetary award by Parliament, and honoured by national institutions such as Trinity House. However, in one important respect Greathead succeeded where Lukin had failed: multiple copies of his lifeboat were built and adopted around the coast of the UK at over thirty locations.

Lukin died in 1834, aged 91, and overlooked for his important contribution to sea safety. His gravestone at Hythe, Kent, states he 'was the first who built a life-boat, and was the original inventor of that principle of safety, by which many lives and much property have been preserved from shipwreck; and he obtained for it the King's patent in the year 1785'.

Henry Greathead's lifeboat.

20

Mirror

The wreck of Halsewell *was so notorious that the King insisted on visiting the site personally*

Halsewell was an East India Company ship. It began its last voyage on 1 January 1786, under Captain Richard Peirce, after embarking final passengers at Deal in Kent. The ship was also carrying a complement of soldiers.

On 3 January a fierce storm arose off the Dorset coast, and *Halsewell* shipped much water as huge waves broke over it. To the captain's consternation there was soon several feet of water in the hold. The crew battled the elements for three days, using sails to try to keep away from the land, working the pumps ceaselessly and eventually cutting away two masts. In its last hours *Halsewell* was driven shorewards despite deploying two anchors. At 2am on 6 January the ship struck the cliffs near St Aldhelm's Head with such violence that people on board were thrown up in the air.

It was pitch dark and cold. Initially, the crew hoped to wait for daylight before abandoning ship but *Halsewell* began breaking apart. Captain Peirce realised there was no hope for his beloved daughters so chose to stay with them and the other female passengers. However, some crewmen and soldiers managed to clamber from the ship to the rocks, although many failed in the attempt. The groaning *Halsewell* suddenly burst asunder, carrying all those left on board to their deaths. There was a loud shriek in which, as one survivor wrote, 'the voice of female distress was lamentably distinguishable'.

Meanwhile, many men sought refuge in a cavern at the base of the steep cliffs, which are around 100 feet high. Others clung to the black rocks wherever they could. However, the merciless pounding of the waves, the icy cold wind and the rising tide meant that many could not hold on for long, and one by one they fell into the stormy sea.

After a few desperate hours, some men tried to clamber up the perpendicular cliff face, but several fell to their deaths. However, the cook and the quartermaster succeeded and raised the alarm. Local vicar Morgan Jones wrote that 'the water as far as the eye could extend, was disfigured with floating carcasses, tables, chairs, casks, and part of every other article in the vessel'. Soon, workers from the local quarry

were on hand to pull up the survivors one by one using ropes. Only seventy-four men were saved from an estimated 286 people on board *Halsewell*. Many bodies were washed ashore locally, but others were found as far away as Christchurch.

It was an infamous wreck and was the subject of contemporary poems, books, music, sermons and even a sound and light show. It was later depicted by artists including Turner and Gillray. George III was so moved by accounts of *Halsewell* that he and his family visited the clifftops to view the scene of the tragedy, and the king wept openly.

The mirror is on display in a local church, and was one of many items retrieved from the wreck in the ensuing days. Perhaps it was used by one of the captain's ill-fated daughters.

The steep Dorset cliffs where the wreck occurred.

21

Iceberg

The heroic survival of those on board Lady Hobart *was a celebrated early nineteenth-century tale*

Many ships have been wrecked as a result of hitting icebergs including, most famously, *Titanic* in 1912. Yet the story of *Lady Hobart* is one of the earliest for which a detailed account is available. An armed mail ship, *Lady Hobart* departed Nova Scotia on 23 June 1803 bound for England under Captain William Fellowes. Three days into the voyage a French schooner was sighted and captured. Its crew was despatched with the prize and into passing English ships bound for Newfoundland, except for the French captain and two crewmates.

On 28 June a storm arose with heavy seas and poor visibility. About one o'clock the next morning *Lady Hobart* struck an iceberg in the darkness with such violence that several crewmen were thrown out of their hammocks. Although they tried to navigate away from the ice mass the ship struck it a second time. The iceberg was enormous – at least twice the height of the ship's main mast and more than a quarter of a mile long. The crew raced to save their vessel: anchors and guns went overboard to lighten it, pumps and buckets evacuated the in-rushing water, and the holes in the ship's hull were covered with sails. But the damage proved too great.

Captain Fellowes ordered the ship's cutter and jolly-boat to be launched. It was dawn, cold and stormy, and they were about 350 miles from Newfoundland. Thankfully, all twenty-nine people on board scrambled into the boats before *Lady Hobart* sank. Their number comprised five

passengers, including Fellowes' wife and two other ladies, and three French prisoners, and the rest were crewmen. Their initial apprehensions were heightened by being surrounded by a large school of whales, but fortunately none struck the boats.

The survivors were crammed into the two small boats with hardly room to move, and the gunwales were only a few inches from the surface of the sea so they were in constant fear of being swamped. It was necessary to bail out constantly. Their provisions were exceedingly meagre: each person was allowed half a biscuit and a glass of wine for the entire first day. Heavy rain soon soaked them, but they rowed the boats and put up a sail when they could. The weather deteriorated repeatedly, and it was extremely cold with sea spray freezing in the air as it flew over the boats. No one was wearing appropriate clothes for an open boat and the inability to

move or even stretch was almost unbearable. A glass of rum fortified them against the cold on the worst days. They prayed often.

On 2 July it was so cold that their hands and feet turned black and almost everyone was unable to move. Twice the two boats became separated by storms but found each other again. Their thirst was intense and some of the crew drank seawater and became delirious. On 3 July the French captain, in a fit of despondency, suddenly leapt overboard and vanished beneath the waves. Another prisoner was so uncontrollable that he had to be lashed down.

After seven days adrift, they sighted land and managed one last effort with the oars. When they were picked up by a schooner they were all so weak that they had to be lifted to safety, and some men later lost fingers and toes because of the cold. Yet by a miracle they had survived.

Contemporary hand-coloured mezzotint of *Lady Hobart* sinking.

22

Flint for a musket

Part of the cargo from the wreck of Earl of Abergavenny

The poet William Wordsworth's brother, John, was a captain for the East India Company. He had commanded *Earl of Abergavenny* on two previous voyages to China, but shortly after commencing his third voyage the vessel was wrecked on 5 February 1805. The valuable cargo included coins, porcelain and wine – which was recovered afterwards – but also a large consignment of flints for military firearms. The flints were an integral part of the weapon's firing mechanism and had to be replaced when worn.

Captain Wordsworth died within sight of the shore. William was deeply distressed by his brother's loss and wrote a number of poems about his feelings, often using his well-known love of nature to try to express himself. None is more melancholic than the *Elegaic Verses in Memory of my Brother, John Wordsworth*, which opens with this stanza:

The Sheep-boy whistled loud, and lo!
That instant, startled by the shock,
The Buzzard mounted from the rock

Deliberate and slow:
Lord of the air, he took his flight;
Oh! Could he on that woeful night
Have lent his wing, my Brother dear,
For one poor moment's space to Thee,
And all who struggled with the Sea,
When safety was so near.

Unfortunately, the events that led to John's death were caused by the incompetence of a pilot sent from Weymouth to navigate the ship. He was late for duty so they missed the best of the tide, and then he took the wrong course, resulting in the ship being stranded on the infamous shingle-bank called The Shambles.

Trapped by the tide, the ship's hull thumped repeatedly against the bank until eventually the hull was breached and water gushed in. When the tide rose, *Earl of Abergavenny* slipped clear and Captain Wordsworth attempted to beach it

in the shallows. Yet the influx of seawater proved too much, overwhelming the pumps. The mate declared: 'We have done all we can, Sir, she will sink in a moment.' The Captain replied, 'It cannot be helped – God's will be done.' At eleven o'clock a heavy sea finished the vessel off: it foundered in an instant, just a mile and a half from safety.

Most of those who survived ran up the rigging: the ship sank upright and when the hull hit the seabed the mast-tops protruded above the waves. From here people could be rescued. There had been more than four hundred people on board and 263 died, including John Wordsworth. His remains were found on the beach near Weymouth several weeks later. Many have attributed a decline in William Wordsworth's creative output to the loss of this much-loved brother.

Flints from the wreck are still washed up on shore or recovered by divers.

Survivors clinging to *Earl of Abergavenny*'s mast-tops.

East India Company token

Salvaged from the wreck of Admiral Gardner *which sank in 1809*

In January 1809 *Admiral Gardner* was sailing from Blackwall on the Thames to Madras with a crew of about one hundred men, carrying a heavy cargo that included iron bars, chains, anchors and cannonballs. Furthermore, the vessel was transporting around 50 tons of copper tokens, such as the one shown here, packed into barrels. These were used as the East India Company's own currency to pay native employees.

On the night of 24 January 1809 *Admiral Gardner* anchored near South Foreland. The wind increased violently and the ship's captain, William Eastfield, was afraid that the ship would be driven onto the Goodwin Sands. The crew could not get all the sails in and they hoped that the anchor cable would hold, but the ship was relentlessly driven in the direction of the Sands. When the tide turned it was anticipated that the ship might avoid running aground but the wind continued to push the ship towards danger. Early on the morning of 25 January white waves were seen breaking in the shallow waters to the lee side of the ship. It was now impossible to save *Admiral Gardner*, but Captain Eastfield ordered the main and mizzen masts to be cut away in an attempt to lighten the vessel. As they were doing this, the ship struck the Goodwin Sands and the sea broke completely over the vessel in great waves.

In the days before the Royal National Lifeboat Institution, those who went to the rescue of stricken ships were volunteers in local boats that were not necessarily designed for survival in rough seas. Boatmen from Deal in Kent gallantly rowed out to try to effect a rescue. The seas were extremely challenging but somehow they eventually managed to save everyone on board *Admiral Gardner* except for one man. Another East India Company ship, *Britannia*, travelling in convoy, was also wrecked and lost seven men.

Both ships broke apart and were scattered and it proved impossible to salvage the contents of either wreck at the time.

The approximate location of the wreck *Admiral Gardner* was located in the mid-1970s when a dredger brought up some of the copper tokens. In the 1980s the wreck was pinpointed more precisely after a local fisherman kept snagging his nets on something. At this stage over a million East India Company tokens were recovered, as well as a complete barrel containing twenty-eight thousand coins. The tokens were termed 'cash' from the Tamil word *Kasu*, meaning a coin.

Message in a bottle

A desperate message washed up after the wreck of Kent *in 1825*

This deeply poignant message was found by a bather in a bottle on Bathsheba beach, Barbados. The short note reads:

The ship *Kent*, Indiaman, is on fire. Elizabeth, Joanna and myself commit our spirits into the hands of our blessed Redeemer – his grace enables us to be quite composed in the awful prospect of entering eternity. DW McGregor.
1st March 1825. Bay of Biscay.

We know from accounts of other shipwrecks that those facing certain death often, understandably, wanted to send a last message to their loved ones, but equally importantly they wanted to explain their fate. No one wants to disappear and leave their family for ever wondering.

Kent was operating as a troop-ship and was bound for India, carrying men of the 31st Regiment of Foot and their families. The officer in command was Lieutenant Colonel Fearon and his second-in-command was Major Duncan McGregor, the calm and devout writer of the message in the bottle.

Not long after leaving the English Channel, a ship's officer went below to secure some loose cargo, but dropped his lantern just as a barrel of spirits burst open. It must have been like someone throwing a petrol bomb. The whole cargo hold was soon furiously ablaze. A fire on a sailing ship of this period was terrifying. The hull and masts were made of wood, and to make matters worse the rigging and decks were soaked with inflammable pitch to waterproof them. The conflagration was soon completely out of control. Major McGregor grabbed a pencil and wrote his brave message at this point because the complete destruction of the ship and the 630 or so people aboard seemed inevitable. He addressed it to his father, John. It was only a matter of time before the ship's gunpowder supplies would be caught in the blaze and then *Kent* would blow up.

However, unexpectedly, rescue was at hand in the form of the brigantine *Cambria*, under Captain William Cook, who saw the smoke and bore down to rescue almost everyone on board, despite the extreme risk. At 2am *Kent* exploded, but *Cambria* managed to return and pick up a further fourteen people from the floating wreckage. Cook's heroic efforts led to the saving of 547 individuals in total, although eighty-one people died (fifty-four soldiers, a woman, twenty children, a seaman, and five boys).

Happily, Major McGregor, his wife and daughter survived the destruction and he was promoted in recognition of his courage and leadership in adversity. His message in a bottle was picked up about eighteen months later and returned to him.

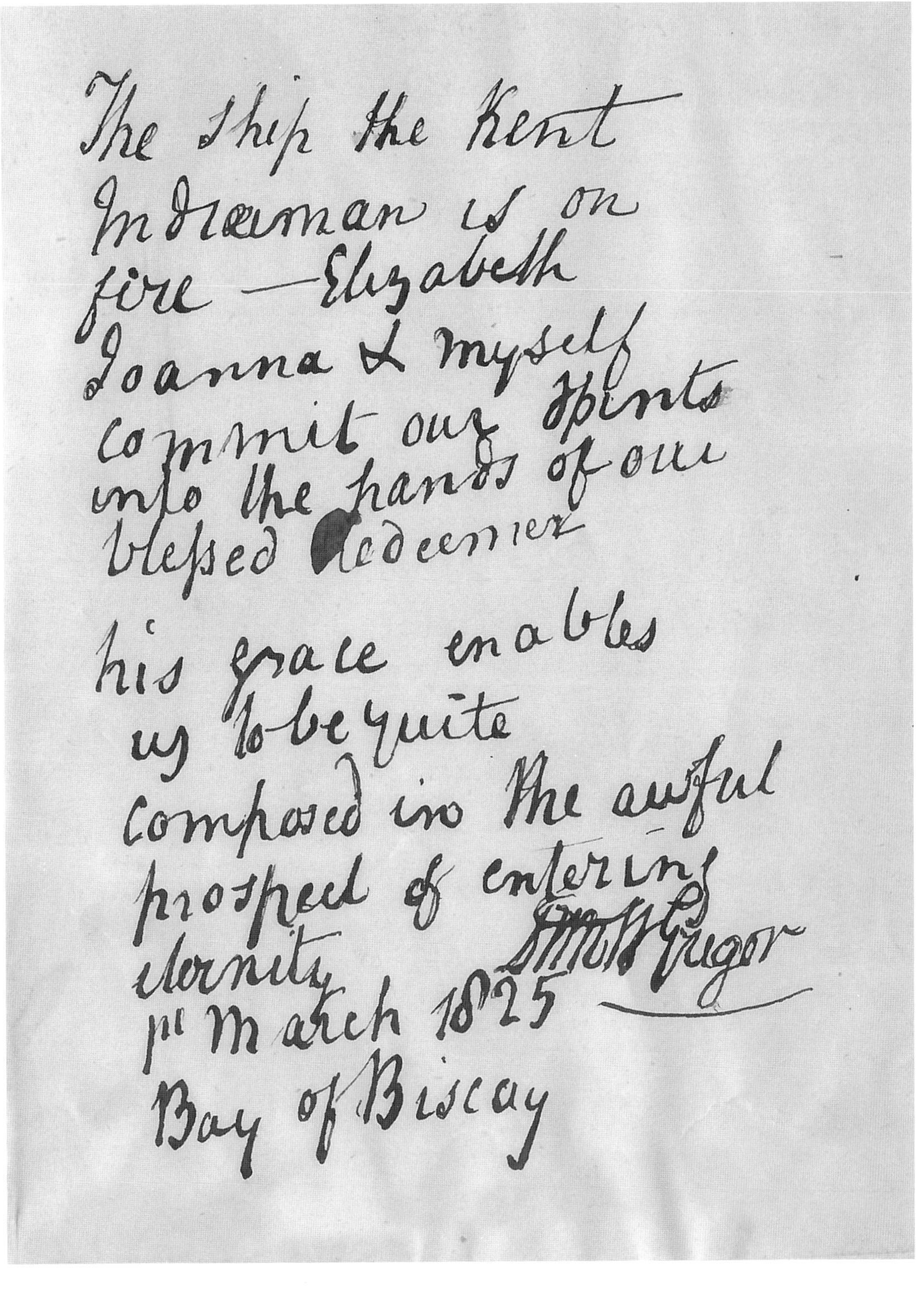

The ship the Kent
Indiaman is on
fire — Elizabeth
Joanna & myself
commit our spirits
into the hands of our
blessed Redeemer

his grace enables
us to be quite
composed in the awful
prospect of entering
eternity   MMacGregor
1st March 1825
Bay of Biscay

25

RNLI gold medal

*From the outset, the RNLI sought to reward bravery when
rescuing people from shipwreck*

In 1822 William Hillary saw at first hand the tragic wreck of HMS *Racehorse* off the coast of the Isle of Man. Crewmen on the ship died but so did local fishermen who tried their best to rescue them, leaving widows and unsupported children. Hillary was moved to suggest that the nation adopt a system of coastal lifeboat stations to ensure that communities

were ready to stage properly organised rescues utilising the best boats and equipment available.

Hillary wrote to the Admiralty, to commercial organisations and to leading politicians and philanthropists urging the creation of a 'national institution for the preservation of lives and property from shipwreck'. His appeals to the Admiralty fell on deaf ears but Hillary persisted with his vision and fortunately secured enthusiastic private backing, enabling the establishment of the *National Institution for the Preservation of Life from Shipwreck* as a charity in 1824. The idea captured the public's attention and the Institution grew rapidly, establishing lifeboat stations all over Britain.

From the start, the Institution was determined to reward those who risked their lives to save others from shipwreck, and began issuing medals. The medals originally bore the head of the monarch on one side and on the reverse a rescue featuring three men helping a fourth into their boat. Its legend 'Let not the deep swallow me up' was taken from Psalm 69. The first ever gold medal was issued in the year of the Institution's foundation, 1824, when coastguard Charles Fremantle courageously swam out from the shore at Christchurch to a Swedish brig that was stranded and breaking up.

By 1854 Queen Victoria was delighted to bestow her patronage on the Institution, and the organisation changed its name to the *Royal National Lifeboat Institution* or RNLI.

Henry Blogg from Cromer, Norfolk, is the most decorated lifeboatman in history, having been awarded the RNLI gold medal three times and the silver medal four times. His first gold medal came in 1917 when he and his crew set out in stormy seas four times to two different wrecks within the space of fourteen hours. In 1927 Henry's second gold medal resulted from spending 28 hours attending a wrecked oil tanker that had broken in half, saving fifteen lives. Finally, in 1941, aged 65, his and three other lifeboats went out to six stranded vessels and between them saved eighty-eight lives in very dangerous conditions. He continued as coxswain of the Cromer lifeboat until he was 71 and received many other awards for bravery.

Henry Blogg meeting the Prince of Wales (later Edward VIII).

26

Diving helmet design

Shipwrecks could be a profitable business for those with the right equipment

John Deane was an intelligent and courageous man, and the story of how he and his brother Charles invented the diving helmet depicted below is fascinating. In the 1820s John was at the location of a fire in a stable where the horses could not be reached because of the flames. A pump was being used to send a jet of water into the blaze but it was insufficient and the fire continued unabated. Suddenly John Deane had a flash of inspiration. Donning a medieval knight's helmet from a suit of armour that he had seen in a building nearby, he inserted the end of the hose that was being used to pump water under the helmet, and asked that the pumping continued so that fresh air would prevent him asphyxiating in the smoke. To everyone's amazement, Deane rescued the horses.

This act of inspiration and bravery set Deane thinking that a modified version of this apparatus might be used for accessing the sea floor. He and his brother designed a metal helmet with glass portholes, and a waterproofed diving suit that came up to the neck inside the helmet. The 'Deane helmet' was open at the bottom and relied upon air being pumped into it to allow the diver to breathe and to stop water coming in. Initial dives were not successful because the large air pocket in the helmet repeatedly unbalanced John when submerged. This was corrected when the brothers adopted shoes weighted with lead.

Early dives in Kent and elsewhere in 1828 and 1829 confirmed the practical and safe application of Deane's diving equipment in deep water, and its utility for salvaging ship's

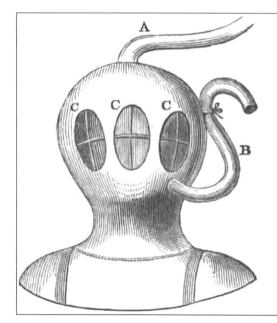

A, pipe by which air forced in.

B, pipe by which air escapes.

C, strong plate-glass windows.

Coat of arms of Bermuda featuring the 1609 wreck of *Sea Venture* (chapter 4)

Left: Cannon salvaged from East India Company ship *Trial*, lost in 1622 (chapter 5)

Below: Beautifully preserved pocket sundial from the 1665 wreck of *London* (chapter 7)

Snuff box made from timbers of HMS *Royal George* which sank in harbour in 1782; the wood was salvaged in 1839 (chapter 17)

Bird-shaped wooden tureen inlaid with shell from Palau – a gift to Captain Wilson of the ill-fated *Antelope* in 1783 (chapter 18)

Mirror found amongst the rocks after the tragic demise of *Halsewell* (chapter 20)

Icebergs have sunk many ships, including *Lady Hobart* in 1803 (chapter 21)

Abandoning the sinking *Lady Hobart*, but worse was to come…

Left: The RNLI's gold medal first awarded in 1824 (chapter 25)

Below: JMW Turner's evocative *Wreckers* painted in about 1833 (chapter 27)

Above: Naval officer's epaulettes discovered on the wreck of HMS *Erebus* probably belonging to third lieutenant James Fairholme (chapter 30)

Right: An idealised portrait of Sir John Franklin, wearing officers' epaulettes

Ralph Sheldon Bond's pocketwatch survived the sinking of HMS *Birkenhead* (chapter 34)

Great white sharks ate many men after HMS *Birkenhead* went down

anchors, cannon and so forth. The brothers were able to establish a commercial business, and John Deane subsequently dived on a number of famous wrecks, including *Mary Rose* and HMS *Royal George*. In each case he was able to salvage valuable historical items which could be sold for profit to an eager audience.

Before the Deanes' invention, people had used diving bells for salvage operations but they were cumbersome and difficult to operate. The diving suit and helmet enabled a man to walk on the seabed to wherever he wished and attach ropes to even very heavy objects so that they might be hauled to the surface. Such was Deane's acclaim that he was hired by the Royal Navy to clear wrecks from Sevastopol harbour during the Crimean War.

Perhaps surprisingly, given his potentially perilous line of work, John Deane lived to a ripe old age for the time, dying aged 84 in Ramsgate.

An early Victorian diver in full dress.

27

Wreckers, *a painting by J. M. W. Turner*

British artists, particular Turner, have long had a fascination with adversity at sea

Joseph Mallord William Turner painted this scene in around 1833. Its full title is *Wreckers – Coast of Northumberland, with a Steam-Boat Assisting a Ship off Shore*. It was one of many works by him featuring the human relationship with the sea, and near the beginning of his career it was subject matter that did much to establish his early reputation.

Appropriately enough, the first oil painting he ever exhibited at the Royal Academy in 1796 was *Fishermen at Sea*, presenting a vulnerable-looking boat in a lively sea at night. The power of the sea, and particularly the battle between people and the waves, was a topic that he returned to repeatedly throughout his life by painting wrecks, or ships in stormy waters. Contemporary commentators noted with approval that Turner's paintings provoked their emotions.

One of his earliest examples of a storm at sea, *The Shipwreck*, was exhibited in 1805. It is not known to depict a real disaster, but it has been suggested that Turner may have been inspired either by the sinking of *Earl of Abergavenny* (see Chapter 22) or by the republication of William Falconer's epic poem (Chapter 15). However, some of his other works are known to represent actual tragedies. In about 1818, for example, he was moved to paint *The Loss of an East Indiaman*, showing the demise of *Halsewell*, a wreck still notorious in the public memory even thirty-two years after it happened (see Chapter 20). Turner's *A Disaster at Sea* (c.1835) illustrated the loss of *Amphitrite* in 1833, in which 108 women and 12 children were lost when a convict ship foundered off the coast of Boulogne.

Wreckers is an oil painting on canvas, and shows the common opportunistic pursuit amongst coastal settlements of retrieving items from a wrecked or abandoned ship. This might include cargo, timber, furniture, fittings and rigging but also items such as jewellery taken from corpses washed ashore. Shipwrecks were so common in the eighteenth and nineteenth centuries that wrecking was an important source of income for some communities, particularly in Cornwall, parts of Scotland, and the shore near the Goodwin Sands.

There is no evidence that wreckers deliberately lured ships ashore on stormy nights in order to wreck them, despite the frequent portrayal of this activity in fiction such as *Jamaica Inn* by Daphne du Maurier. However, sometimes it could get out of hand. As far back as the 1370s, Edward III prosecuted a hundred people from Dorset who robbed the ship *Welfare* of its cargo and molested its crew. The ship had run aground but had not been abandoned, so could not legally be boarded. Even the abbot of the local monastery was convicted.

Tighter legal controls on what was formerly known as 'wrecking' led to it evolving into what is now termed marine salvage.

28

Grace Darling's boat

The boat used to save shipwreck victims in one of the most famous sea rescues of all time

Grace Darling lived with her parents at the Longstone lighthouse, on the Farne Islands off the coast of Northumberland. Her father, William, was the lighthouse keeper. On the morning of 7 September 1838 Grace was looking out of an upper window during a storm when she spotted the remains of a ship with a small group of people desperately clinging to the wreckage. The vessel was the paddle-steamer SS *Forfarshire*, a local ship carrying sixty-three people, which had struck Big Harcar Rock during the night after its engines failed. The ship was breaking apart.

Grace roused her father and they tried to decide what to do. There was no one else at the remote lighthouse apart from Grace's elderly mother, and the survivors would soon die if they were not rescued. It must have been an incredibly tough decision for William Darling to risk his daughter's life by venturing out onto those stormy seas. He would also have weighed the dangers of him abandoning the lighthouse, which had to be maintained during the bad weather to alert other ships to the rocks. In the end they agreed to go, with 22-year-old Grace credited as taking the initiative to venture forth.

They used the lighthouse's coble, a small open boat about 20 feet long, and rowed a roundabout route to the wreck to take advantage of as much natural shelter from the elements as they could.

Nonetheless, it was an arduous haul but William had banked on rescuing people who could help them row back.

When they reached the wreck, William faced the most difficult moment of all: he had to leave his daughter alone to manage the coble while he boarded the wreck. He quickly assessed the situation. There were nine people left alive, but there was no room in the coble to take all of them at once, so they had to make two trips. Fortunately they were successful, and the victims were cared for in the cramped conditions of the lighthouse for two days until the weather abated.

The news of Grace's heroism spread rapidly. The family were soon beset by reporters, painters and tourists. Grace was sent many gifts, including from Queen Victoria, as well as rewards for bravery: she was the first woman to receive an RNLI medal. Sadly, however, she was not able to enjoy her celebrity status for long, dying of tuberculosis just four years later.

Grace Darling's boat was saved for the nation and is little changed since the events of 1838. The photograph on the previous page was taken at the Great International Fisheries Exhibition in London in 1883 where the Shipwrecked Fishermen & Mariners Royal Benevolent Society brought together many items related to Grace to help raise funds. The boat now has pride of place in the RNLI Grace Darling Museum in Bamburgh.

Grace and her father rowing out to the rescue.

29

Membership ticket for the Shipwrecked Fishermen and Mariners' Royal Benevolent Society

Founded in 1839 to support shipwrecked seafarers in their hour of greatest need

On 21 October 1838 a calamitous storm descended upon eleven fishing vessels from the village of Clovelly in Devon. The ships were so badly beaten about by wind and waves that only two returned to port, and twenty-one men lost their lives. When he read of this incident, Charles Gee Jones drew it to the attention of his employer John Rye, for whom he acted as servant. This incident came only six weeks after Grace Darling's celebrated rescue, and they agreed that there should be better welfare for the families of seafarers who died.

Plaque at Clovelly marking the Society's foundation.

Membership token bearing Nelson's head, that was worn around the neck.

Assisted by Sir Jahleel Brenton, governor of the Hospital for Seamen at Greenwich, Jones and Rye managed to generate enough capital to establish an organisation to achieve their aims. Initially they had to go door-to-door in Bath, asking for donations, but support gathered pace. The Shipwrecked Fishermen and Mariners' Benevolent Society was founded remarkably quickly, with its inaugural public meeting held on 21 February 1839, only four months' after the Clovelly wrecks. Queen Victoria soon became its patron.

Many shipwreck victims were stranded after getting ashore. Often cold, naked, starving and penniless, they had to rely on begging to get home again. Fishermen and merchant seamen who subscribed to the Society at a rate of 2 shillings and 6 pence per year were promised clothing, food and transport via a network of the Society's agents should they ever be shipwrecked. It was the first time that British seafarers had access to nationwide welfare of this kind. Previous to this, local people might sometimes donate clothes or food to victims, but since coastal communities were often impoverished, this was not guaranteed.

However, the Society went further than this. It recognised that the loss of a seafaring husband almost invariably plunged his wife and family into immediate destitution. Hence another part of the insurance provided by the annual subscription was to 'preserve the widow and orphans from want and distress'. This took many forms, such as paying the rent, teaching the widow an occupation so that she could earn money, or providing fishing equipment to a young son so that he might support his mother and siblings.

It was necessary for seafarers to prove to the Society's agents that they were members. To this end, they were issued with two items. The first was a member's ticket that was kept at home so that dependents could use it to claim their relief if needed. The second proof of entitlement was a metal token that was tied around the seaman's neck like a pendant so that hopefully it would survive a shipwreck. It bore a bust of Nelson and carried his famous message 'England expects every man will do his duty'. Both membership items were replaced annually with new dated versions.

The Society was very popular and within ten years had twenty-six thousand members. It literally made the difference between life and death for many seafarers and their families in the nineteenth century. The Society still exists today, but as a charity rather than a membership organisation, and mainly supports retired or disabled seafarers from the fishing industry and Merchant Navy, and their widows or partners. It uses decommissioned sea mines as collection boxes for donations, and these are a familiar sight in coastal towns.

30

An officer's epaulettes

An artefact from two polar expedition ships that disappeared in 1846

In May 1845 Sir John Franklin led HMS *Erebus* and HMS *Terror* on an expedition to try to find a long-sought Northwest Passage linking the Atlantic Ocean to the Pacific via Arctic Canada. By September 1846 both ships with their crew of about 130 men were iced in, unable to move. This was a dangerous situation and the crew would have known that they might not survive. The ice thickens as the winter advances, and it could gradually crush trapped vessels. This was a familiar cause of ship losses in locations such as the Baltic, and it was to be the cause of Ernest Shackleton losing his ship *Endurance* during his Antarctic exploration in 1915.

What happened to Franklin's polar team is not clear because no one survived to tell the tale. The mission had been expected to be of long duration and so the Admiralty did not begin searching for Franklin's 'Lost Expedition' until 1848, but many searches were made over the ensuing years. Interviews with local Inuit revealed that the crew had left their ships but had slowly perished, even resorting to cannibalism at the end.

In 1859 a note found under a cairn revealed that Franklin himself had died on 11 June 1847, and twenty-three others by April 1848. At this time, having been imprisoned in the ice for more than eighteen months, the rest of the crew, comprising 105 people, abandoned

their collapsing ships in an attempt to walk to safety.

In the 1980s remains of some of the crew were found on land. Analysis of their remains suggested that they probably died of a combination of factors, including malnutrition, chest infections and poisoning from the lead solder used to seal their tins of food. Study of their bones confirmed Inuit reports of cannibalism.

The ships themselves remained undiscovered until 2014, when Parks Canada's Underwater Archaeology Team located *Erebus*, and in 2016 the wreck of *Terror* was found. The two vessels were about 45 miles apart. *Terror* is the most complete and still holds china sitting on shelves in the mess, and bottles standing upright in cupboards.

Underwater archaeologists working on *Erebus* have recovered many beautifully preserved items, including a hairbrush that still holds some human hairs, an accordion, ceramics, buttons and even part of the ship's wheel. The epaulettes shown on the previous page were worn atop the shoulders and were part of a lieutenant's dress uniform; being made partly of gold, they were one of the most expensive elements of the outfit. They were found in a cabin that may have belonged to third lieutenant James Fairholme.

Hopefully, the continued exploration and analysis of these wrecks and their contents will finally reveal what happened to the ships, why they were so far apart, and if anyone remained on board at the time of their sinking.

A somewhat idealised portrait of Sir John Franklin, wearing officers' epaulettes.

31

Lisle family gravestone

A tragedy at Cullercoats, Northumberland, took seven men to their deaths in 1848

George Lisle was a pilot, a navigator of the treacherous waters of the entrance to the river Tyne. He operated a pilot vessel with his two sons, George Jr and Robert, his brother Robert Lisle, his brother-in-law Robert Clarke, and two friends, James Stocks and Charles Pearson.

The clear conditions on Wednesday, 2 February 1848 excited no fears amongst the local community, although the sea was running high

and the wind was squally. Several vessels out at sea hoisted flags to request a pilot to navigate them to a safe moorage up-river. George Lisle and his crew launched from the beach, but just a short distance from the shore a large wave broke over them and swamped the boat. The next wave turned the vessel over, drowning two occupants, whilst the remainder clung desperately to the bottom of their craft.

All this could be seen clearly from the shore and people rushed to the beach. Boats were launched to provide aid but the strong onshore wind prevented them getting close enough. As families and friends alike watched in horror, the sea pounded the stricken boat, tearing the men away one by one. Robert Lisle was only 24 years old; he lashed himself to the mast to try to save himself, but eventually even he was ripped away.

The last man, James Stocks, was a strong swimmer and as the drifting vessel neared the rocks he stripped off his jacket and waistcoat and struck out for land. He was so close to safety that his brother shouted to him 'Jim, swim ashore', but poor James was exhausted and called out

'I'm done, I'm done', and after a short struggle he slipped beneath the waves. This whole awful scene played out in front of the distraught wives, children and parents of the unfortunate victims in less than an hour.

Notwithstanding their unspeakable grief, six wives and fourteen children under 11 were immediately left destitute because the families' main breadwinners had died. Three wives were heavily pregnant at the time. Fortunately, their close-knit community rallied around: a collection raised a significant sum and most of the bereaved had family who could support them.

The majority of disasters described in this book are wrecks of substantial vessels that left hundreds of families grieving. However, it is important to acknowledge events such as this one at Cullercoats, which devastated a smaller number of households. Such tragedies did not make the national newspapers. Yet they were common, and most coastal communities have graves and memorials that remind us of the risks to which fishermen, pilots, lifeboatmen, crews of coastal ferries and others were regularly exposed.

A Victorian pilot with his son; it was an occupation that often ran in families.

32

Handwritten account of two storms at sea

Captain Parish's journal describes events that tore his ship apart in 1848

Sutlej was a an East Indiaman – a large commercial sailing vessel built for conveying cargo rather than for speed, and armed with cannon against pirates. Alfred

Parish was *Sutlej*'s new captain when in spring 1848 he set sail for London from Madras in India. The cargo hold was full and he had a large number of passengers, many of whom were

The following account is partly extracted from the Log of the Ship Sutlej on her Voyage to England from Calcutta & Madras —

April 1st 1848 Midnight — Blowing a furious Gale from N. W. tremendous Sea rising — Ship. Lying to —

3 A.M. Sea increasing and rolling in over all — filling the Decks — Ship. staggering under it — & clearing herself with difficulty. Decided on bearing up —

Whilst loosing the Main topsail & fore sail & setting fore top mast stay sail a tremendous Sea struck her on the bow. & broke the Bowsprit close to the Knights head — Put the Helm up but before the Ship could pay off the Bowsprit came alongside — The Foremast rolled over to Seaward — The Main mast fell over the Lee Quarter — & the Mizen Mast over the Stern — All three going close to the deck and taking three Quarter Boats with them —

Considering the Ship in danger from the Wreck commenced cutting away every thing. The Ship rolling fearfully. A gang of Soldiers of HM's 50 keeping the Pumps sucking & bailing out from the Lower Deck — The Sea rushing in through one of the Stern Ports which had been stove in and also through the Starboard Quarter Galley door & down the Poop Skylights.

soldiers from the Queen's Own 50th Regiment of Foot. All went well until midnight on 1 April, when a furious gale arose. Parish described the situation at 3am:

> Sea increasing and rolling in over all, filling the decks. Ship staggering under it, and clearing herself with difficulty. Decided on bearing up.
>
> Whilst loosing the main topsail and foresail and setting foretopmast staysail, a tremendous sea struck her on the bow and broke the bowsprit close to the knights-head. Put the helm up, but before the ship could pay off the bowsprit came alongside. The foremast rolled over the leeward, the main mast fell over the lee quarter, and the mizzen mast over the stern. All three going close to the deck and taking three quarter boats with them.
>
> Considering the ship in danger from the wreckage, commenced cutting away everything. The ship rolling fearfully. A gang of soldiers of HM's 50 keeping the pumps sucking, and bailing out from the lower deck.

By 10am the weather was moderating but the ship had no masts and was badly damaged. It took two days to clear the wreckage away and to erect 'jury masts' – stumpy masts made from spare timber which carried just enough sail to get *Sutlej* under way. To ease the pressure on the weakened ship, Parish ordered four hundred sacks of cargo to be jettisoned. Crew and passengers came together on Sunday to thank God for sparing them. But it was not over yet.

On 4 April *Sutlej* was beset by a hurricane. Sails were torn away, the maindeck guns went over the side, and the ship laboured dreadfully as giant waves repeatedly buried it under water. The log-like vessel rolled and nose-dived into heavy seas for two days, and Parish wrote that at any moment he expected the hull to give way, allowing the sea to gush in. Mercifully that didn't happen. Another four hundred sacks of cargo (mainly rice) went overboard, and the weather slowly improved: by 7 April it was only a fresh gale, and next day land was sighted. At 7pm on 10 April they anchored at Cape Town. By some miracle they had survived.

Captain Parish totted up the losses. One sailor had fallen overboard, another had lost an arm, and others were severely injured. Not including the loss of cargo and provisions, the damage to the ship was estimated at a staggering £8,000.

Not every ship broken by the elements is lost, but it had been a near run thing for *Sutlej*.

33

Commemorative brass plaque

The steamship Amazon *caught fire and ran out of control in 1851*

It seems surprising that a ship can burn to destruction when surrounded by water. Yet the sad and frightening story of RMS *Amazon* illustrates how a fire at sea can rapidly become unmanageable.

Amazon was a mail-ship. It had a wooden hull, not the iron or steel that was becoming standard, and utilised a pair of paddlewheels amidships to move it through the water, rather than propellers. The ship left Southampton for the Caribbean on 2 January 1851 on her maiden voyage, under Captain William Symons. *Amazon* had a crew of 112 and embarked fifty passengers as well as the mail.

The ship's engines kept over-heating, necessitating water to be pumped over them to cool down. Then, at about 12.45 in the morning on 4 January, one of the officers saw flames and smoke issuing from the engine room. An engineer tried to stop the engines but the smoke in the engine room was too dense to allow him to reach the controls. The firemen that heaved coal into the ship's furnaces had had their backs to the conflagration and did not see it until too late. By the time hoses were brought out to pump water over the flames, it was too hot and smoky to get near enough to have any effect. One survivor described the flames as 'a great wave of fire, before which no man could stand and live'. Within a few minutes the centre of the ship was engulfed.

Captain Symons put the ship before the wind. This carried the flames away from the passengers and crew, who were by now all towards the stern. However, the wind was approaching gale force so the burning ship raced headlong at full speed. They could not extinguish the fire; they could not disengage the engines; and the ship's speed made launching any lifeboat dangerous. Nonetheless, some terrified passengers did attempt it; this first boat turned over and they were all lost. The captain ran to save another boat from the flames but his hair and clothing caught fire and he had to back off. Two of the remaining boats were now ablaze, others were accidentally damaged during the haste to launch them. There were some terrible scenes: people were horribly burned, and one couple leapt into the flames to hasten their end.

A second boat was not lowered correctly and pitched all its occupants into the sea. The next boat was swamped by a wave that washed away almost everyone on board. Eventually, two boats were successfully despatched, one of which leaked badly. The survivors watched *Amazon*'s masts topple and then the gunpowder magazine exploded. Shortly afterwards, the ship went down.

Mercifully, somewhere between 105 and 115 people were somehow saved – picked up from the water or from *Amazon*'s boats by several ships in the vicinity shortly after the sinking.

The ill-fated *Amazon*.

34

Pocketwatch belonging to Ralph Shelton Bond

A personal item that survived the tragic ordeal of HMS Birkenhead

Ralph Shelton Bond had the rank of cornet in the 12th Lancers, equivalent to a second lieutenant today. On 26 February 1852 he was aboard the troopship *Birkenhead*, carrying soldiers and some civilian passengers. En route to the Eastern Cape, the ship's captain, Robert Salmond, hugged the coastline to ensure a speedy voyage. Unhappily, the ship ran onto uncharted rocks at night near Danger Point.

The resulting in-rush of water drowned many soldiers in their sleeping quarters. Poor maintenance meant that some lifeboats were not usable and another was swamped during launch, leaving only three boats for evacuation. As the water rose, Bond raced below decks to save two children who had been left behind. Famously, the order was given for men to stand aside to allow 'Women and children first!' It is widely held to be the origin of this phrase. Shortly after they departed, the ship began to break up and Captain Salmond gave the order to abandon ship. Lieutenant Colonel Seton, in overall command of the soldiers, entreated them not to board the boats as they might swamp them.

His men obeyed him and bravely stayed at their posts. Cornet Bond shook hands with his fellow officers and bade them farewell, then suddenly the remains of the ship lurched, split and heeled over, pitching men into the sea.

Fortunately, *Birkenhead's* main-topmast remained standing above water and men scrambled up this as a place of refuge. A few men in the water were picked up by the boats; others, including Bond, managed to swim ashore, many using bits of floating wreckage to help them. A few men found large enough pieces to use as rafts. Horrible to relate, many were eaten by sharks, which surrounded the struggling men in great numbers. The great white shark is particularly common in these waters. It was a long and arduous swim of about 3 miles for Bond but he did have an inflatable lifevest to assist him. Two men swimming alongside him suddenly disappeared with a shriek, having been taken by sharks.

Approaching the shore, there were new dangers – violent surf threatened to crush the survivors against the jagged rocks, and great quantities of seaweed entangled Bond, so exhausting him that he nearly didn't make it. Bond was in the water for about three hours, and the pocketwatch shown on the previous page was with him. Soon after struggling ashore he found that his beloved horse had swum to the beach as well, and Bond knew he would live. Approximately sixty-eight men reached land with him. Eventually the alarm was raised, but not until many men, often virtually naked, had had to endure a long walk through the inhospitable and baking African sun to seek help.

Meanwhile *Birkenhead's* boats, with about seventy-eight people aboard, were picked up by a schooner which raced to Danger Point; it also rescued around forty men still clinging to the mast. One man was later picked up after thirty-eight hours afloat on a piece of wreckage. There were 193 survivors – including all the women and children – from a total of around 640 who had been on board.

The Danger Point area is notorious for great white sharks.

35

Ship's anchor

*Sometimes the loss of cargo and possessions in a wreck had a
major impact on those affected*

Ships that served the world's more remote communities were, quite literally, lifelines in the past. As well as workers and settlers, they might bring livestock, seeds, agricultural equipment, essential raw materials, textiles, building supplies and so forth. So shipwrecks affecting these places could potentially have an impact beyond any loss of life. In the mid-nineteenth century Western Australia was one such comparatively isolated location.

Unfortunately, this part of the coast was prone to shipwrecks because there are many hazards to navigate.

Eglinton was a barque – a large sailing vessel – that had sailed from Gravesend for Fremantle, Western Australia, where its arrival was keenly awaited. On 3 September 1852 the ship's captain told his passengers that they would see Australia the following morning, but did little to anticipate an imminent landfall. At 9.45pm, during a party to celebrate one passenger's birthday, the look-out cried 'breakers ahead!' and immediately afterwards *Eglinton* struck a reef. Fortunately, the ship was then carried out of the breakers onto an inner reef that was more protected, about a mile from shore. Had the ship stuck on the outer reef it would have been pounded to pieces and everyone on board almost certainly killed.

The ship was aground and stable, but clearly this situation was frightening for the passengers, especially since it was the middle of the night. They had to wait several nervous hours until daylight before they could try to leave the ship. Adopting an 'every man for himself' approach, regrettably some of the crew took to plundering the passengers' baggage and stealing valuable items such as jewellery. This only heightened the poor passengers' anxieties. They were stranded about 50 miles north of Perth, so they knew that help might not come quickly.

The next morning evacuation was attempted, but two boats were dashed to pieces, leaving only one to ferry people ashore. Some of the passengers and the captain did not leave until the following day when the boatswain, who was drunk, threw the ship's chronometer into the sea and was drowned when he jumped in after it. On another occasion the boat turned over and tipped all its passengers into the water, and as a result one unfortunate woman was drowned. These, however, were the only two casualties from the wreck. The passengers were marooned without shelter and were short of water, but were eventually conveyed to Fremantle after the alarm was raised by a local herdsman.

Some of the cargo was saved, especially a consignment of gold coins, but much that had been eagerly anticipated by colonial families for so many months was irretrievably lost. The new settlers also lost all that they had brought with them. It was undoubtedly a major setback for many. Some of the ship's contents, including the anchor shown on the previous page, were retrieved by archaeologists in the 1970s.

Eglinton was a barque and would have looked similar to this vessel.

36

Cork life jacket

Also known as the lifevest or life preserver, it was invented for the RNLI in 1854

Personal flotation devices of various kinds existed in the eighteenth century, but were not widely adopted or standardised. Dr John Wilkinson described the potential benefits of cork life preservers as early as 1765 in his book *Seaman's Preservation from Shipwreck, Diseases, and Other Calamities Incident to Mariners*. However, the invention of the modern type of life jacket is credited to an officer in the Royal Navy, John Ross Ward, who was an Inspector of Lifeboats for the RNLI.

A range of materials were tested by the RNLI to manufacture flotation devices, including rushes and horse hair, balsa wood and inflatable canvas bags, but each of them had significant problems. The buoyancy of rushes and horse hair was not long-lasting, balsa was expensive and canvas bags were too easily punctured. Cork generally met all the criteria for success: it was hardwearing, cheap, easily available and did not become waterlogged.

Blocks of cork were sewn onto a canvas vest. Bigger blocks were used on the chest and back, and smaller blocks (or none) at the sides so that they didn't impede the arm movements needed to row, grab a rope or paddle through the water. Even so, the jacket was bulky and quite heavy.

Ward's design kept a person floating head uppermost in the water, and it could be put on quickly. The intention was that lifeboatmen would wear them on duty, but additionally they would be carried on lifeboats to pass over the heads of shipwreck survivors.

The idea of wearing a life jacket met with initial resistance in some quarters. Once someone fell in the water, it was widely held amongst many seafarers that attempts to swim or stay afloat after a shipwreck simply prolonged the agony, and that a speedy end was preferable. At the same time there were other flotation devices in use that might be preferred, and some people considered that in the heat of action the new bulky life jacket would simply get in the way.

Henry Freeman.

However, a dramatic illustration of the life jacket's ability to preserve life came in 1861. The Whitby lifeboat was called out on multiple occasions to various wrecks during a ferocious storm. During the final rescue attempt a large wave lifted the lifeboat and threw everyone aboard into the violent sea. Henry Freeman was on his first ever call-out and was the only one wearing an RNLI life jacket, which had been donated to the crew. He was the only one who survived. This tragic loss of brave men helped to promote the benefits of life jackets, and ensured they were more widely used. Henry received an RNLI silver medal for his bravery and later became coxswain of the Whitby lifeboat.

Life jackets began to be adopted for passenger use on liners as well. The cork versions were phased out by the RNLI at the beginning of the twentieth century to make way for a new type created in 1904 filled with the plant material kapok.

37

Lifebuoy

Although invented in about 1840, they weren't widely used until the RNLI adopted them in 1855

A constructive idea or invention does not necessarily speak for itself; it often requires a powerful advocate. The creation of the lifebuoy is a good example of this. The lifebuoy was invented by Thomas Kisbee, who was a lieutenant in the Royal Navy. He served fifteen years in the coastguard service, where he became familiar with that organisation's lifesaving role, and seems to have developed the lifebuoy towards the end of his time there in about 1840. His idea was to create a hollow ring of cork wrapped in canvas that a person in the water could put over their head to keep afloat. With a line attached, it could be thrown to someone who was drowning, or to an exhausted shipwreck victim, to enable them to be hauled to safety.

The invention was known for many years as the Kisbee Ring, but is now more familiar on ships and near dangerous waterways around the world as the lifebuoy. Yet although use of this inexpensive device seems to be common sense, it was not widely taken up at sea until the RNLI adopted it as a standard piece of equipment in 1855.

The resourceful Kisbee even went one stage further. He recognised that when a line was

passed to a shipwreck to try to get people ashore or onto a second ship, it was difficult for even seasoned sailors to make their way along it in the stormy conditions that often prevailed. If sailors found it hard, it was near impossible for many passengers. There were various ways around this problem, using devices such as a bosun's chair or similar. A bosun's chair was usually a short plank of wood suspended from a pulley system, upon which a person could sit and be pulled to safety along a rope. However, it required the individual to hang on for dear life to avoid slipping off, and it was consequently less suited to injured people; also, if the line sagged under the water or snapped they could drown.

Kisbee adapted his ring to the purpose and invented the breeches buoy. At the time his creation was often termed 'petticoat breeches' because it looked a little like an oversized lady's undergarment. The device consisted of a large canvas bag in which a person sat with their legs poking through two holes in the bottom. This was suspended from a lifebuoy placed under the armpits so that the individual would remain afloat if the line dipped into the water or broke.

Both of Kisbee's inspired inventions have enabled people to survive drowning, or to be removed from shipwrecks one at a time in greater safety, and have saved thousands of lives at sea.

Breeches buoy being demonstrated.

38

Gold nugget

Many gold prospectors were lost in the infamous wreck of Royal Charter *in 1859*

Even today, the Anglesey coast still sometimes reveals valuable reminders of the loss of *Royal Charter*. The many gold-diggers on board had been prospecting in Australia and, although most of them died when the ship went down, their precious finds were dispersed across a wide area and continue to be found by divers and beachcombers. In 2012 Britain's biggest ever gold nugget was found by a diver. Weighing 97g, it was worth around £50,000 and was part of an estimated £120million of gold (by modern reckoning) that had been on board the ship.

Royal Charter left Melbourne, Australia, in late August and made a speedy passage to Ireland. However, as the ship headed for its final destination, Liverpool, a violent gale erupted on the night of 25 October while the vessel was off the Welsh coast. Captain Thomas Taylor made valiant efforts to save the ship. He sent up signal rockets but no help came; he deployed both anchors but their chains snapped. He tried to use the power of *Royal Charter*'s engines to get away from the land but it was all in vain even when, in desperation, he cut down the ship's masts. The storm had now reached hurricane force and the ship was propelled inexorably shorewards. It soon hit a sandbank, but initially remained intact.

With astonishing bravery a Maltese seaman, Guze Ruggier (but known as Joseph Rogers), volunteered to get a rope ashore and scrambled over the side. He was successful, and with the assistance of local people from the village of Moelfre on Anglesey, there seemed hope of some passengers escaping the wreck. Unfortunately, the ladies who assembled on deck to be roped ashore were all washed overboard by a large wave. Then, suddenly, the rising tide lifted *Royal Charter* off its sandbank and hurled it against the adjacent rocks. The crew frantically attempted to launch lifeboats but they were soon smashed. Within minutes the whole ship broke apart.

Around forty men survived the wreck. The precise death toll is impossible to ascertain but was probably about 450 people. It is said that many of those who drowned were carried to their deaths by the weight of gold hidden about their person or sewn into their clothes for safekeeping. Gold and dead bodies washed ashore in profusion, and some tiny local churchyards were almost overwhelmed. It is alleged that local people made fortunes from their finds of gold, but much of it, carried as cargo, was formally retrieved shortly afterwards.

One passenger who survived against the odds was James Russell. He stood on the ship's stern with his wife and two daughters, separated from the bows by a yawning chasm 'into which every moment human beings were dropping, or being driven by the waves'. The family clung to the ship's rail. They said 'goodbye' to each other, expecting to die. They tried to stick together but James was washed overboard; the next thing he knew, a hand grabbed his and hauled him ashore. Then he passed out. Agonisingly, he had to identify the body of his ten-year-old daughter a few days later. The bodies of his wife and younger daughter were never found.

Many other ships foundered during the hurricane of 25/26 October 1859, which soon became known as the 'Royal Charter storm'.

Guze Ruggier, who bravely swam ashore with a rope.

James Russell, who miraculously survived.

39

Wreck chart for the British Isles

Board of Trade diagram from 1859 illustrating that shipwrecks were common in this era

It is alarming to learn of the frequency of shipwrecks in the past. It might be assumed that the nineteenth-century tragedies described in this book, for example, were simply occasional, isolated events. But that is not the case. The Board of Trade was the Victorian government department responsible for merchant shipping and regularly published an annual register of shipwrecks. The chart shown on the next page is their map illustrating the distribution of a total 1,416 wrecks and strandings which occurred on the coast of the British Isles in 1859 alone. This equates to an average of twenty-seven incidents every week – an appalling statistic. Each little circle or cross on the map represents a single wreck.

Not every wreck or stranding resulted in what was called a 'total loss', because some ships were refloated, salvaged or limped into port to be repaired. There were also cases in which the ship was lost but its cargo was saved. In 1859 the total losses amounted to 527, which is still ten wrecks per week. The human cost was great. The crews of these 1,416 wrecks amounted to 10,538 persons, of whom 3,977 were in imminent peril of dying. Lifeboats saved 2,332 of these, but 1,645 people drowned. Again, it is when this figure is expressed as a weekly statistic that the number hits home: thirty-two people died in a shipwreck every week in 1859. By coincidence, this figure is the same as the number of people who died in the infamous *Costa Concordia* disaster in 2012, in which a cruise ship ran aground and capsized on the coast of Italy. This frightening incident attracted worldwide media coverage, to some extent because of the rarity of events like this in the modern world. Yet in 1859, there was the equivalent of a '*Costa Concordia*' every week on the coast of Britain, at least in terms of the death toll.

The Board of Trade analysed their figures exhaustively. As might be expected, more ships were lost between October and March, when the weather was likely to be bad, than in the other six months of the year, and wrecks were most common at night. Understandably, older ships were more prone to be wrecked, and the 1859 figures include sixty-four ageing veterans that were more than fifty years old, and one that was over a century old!

However, the Board of Trade was keen to stress that the number of vessels departing from British ports in 1859 was 300,580 (including those that left the same port on more than one occasion), and Britain was the centre of world trade so its waterways were exceptionally busy. So it's not surprising that collision was a significant factor in many wrecks. The total cost of these wrecks, comprising vessels and their cargoes, was estimated at about £2million – a colossal sum in 1859.

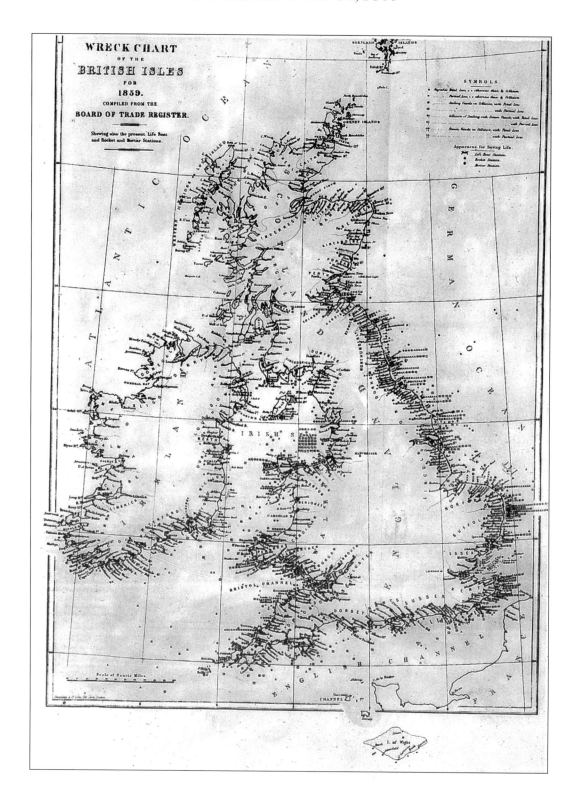

40

Ceramic commemorative mug

Remembering the loss of SS London *– a notorious Victorian catastrophe in 1866*

These days it would be unthinkable to mark a tragedy such as a motorway pile-up or plane crash by issuing commemorative china. However, in Victorian times, disasters where many people lost their lives were viewed differently. In an era long before television or the internet, when a high proportion of the population could not read

or write, it was considered important to ensure that catastrophic events such as the sinking of SS *London* were commemorated and not forgotten. A mug like this was not intended as a ghoulish trinket, but as a physical reminder of those who had died: a way of honouring the lost in an enduring way.

Shortly after beginning only its third voyage to Australia in 1866, the luxury steamship *London* sank in a ferocious storm in the Bay of Biscay. A hatch cover on the maindeck was ripped away, so that the iron ship filled with water like a bathtub. The wreck became notorious because of the heavy death toll and the high social status of many of the people who drowned. Yet its fame also stemmed from the fact that the terrified

Reverend Daniel Draper.

passengers did not attempt to abandon ship, and instead took refuge in prayer, the Bible and the stoical Christian leadership offered by the clergymen on board. In particular, the Reverend Daniel Draper worked tirelessly to prepare the passengers to 'meet their maker'.

Nineteen people did manage to escape, crammed into one of the ship's boats, but at the time their chances of survival in the tiny ship's cutter were deemed so slim that few passengers were willing to join them. When rescued, the occupants of the cutter included just three male passengers and sixteen crewmen. Seafaring records were not always accurate in the 1860s, but it is known that more than 240 people died when SS *London* sank.

The public reacted with disbelief, and the Victorian equivalent of the media industry went into operation. The *Western Times* proclaimed: 'Many years have elapsed since we have had to record a disaster at sea so terrible.' It is a mark of the wreck's impact that the story stayed in the press for months. Within weeks of the shipwreck, a commemorative book was issued that included illustrations of the ship going down, interviews, a list of victims, and a clear message about the triumph of Christian faith and courage over death. A large number of poems were written and published as well – many of them truly awful – and illustrations of the shipwreck were sold. The mug shown on the previous page, with its inscription *The Unfortunate London*, was accompanied by similar ceramic plates and jugs.

Individuals were remembered too. In particular, the heroic Reverend Draper was honoured by a lifeboat being named after him, as well as a public monument, the Draper Memorial Church in Adelaide, and a scholarship fund for young Christians; a road in central Melbourne still bears his name.

41

Autograph of John King

An admirer meets a shipwreck celebrity in 1866

John King became well-known as one of the few survivors of the SS *London* tragedy (chapter 40). His skill in handling a small open boat without a tiller in stormy seas ensured that the occupants survived and he emerged as a hero. The text around his signature here was written by an unknown autograph-hunter, and reads:

The handwriting of the steersman of the small boat, containing 19 souls, who were saved from the wreck of the London. But for the most able exertions of John King (he had only a small piece of wood to steer with) none would have survived to tell the mournful story of that most fearful shipwreck. The above signature and the names of the three vessels in which he has served, all of which have been wrecked, were written by request at the Mansion House, January 1866.

King was an able seaman (AB) on *London*, but the two other shipwrecks that he survived were *Alma* and *Duncan Dunbar*.

Alma was a barque wrecked near Port Robe, South Australia, in 1861. While the ship's captain was ashore, the crew began unloading ballast but a hurricane blew up from nowhere. *Alma*'s anchor chain parted and the high winds propelled the vessel onto rocks. The crew's situation was desperate: they were trapped on a ship that would soon be smashed to pieces by the sea and wind. The local lifeboat service used a rocket to get a line on board, and all twenty-four crewmen, including John King, were warped off one by one using a pulley system. It had been touch and go: within two hours *Alma* was matchwood.

John King's second wreck was *Duncan Dunbar*, a passenger ship which ran aground off the coast of Brazil in 1865. It happened at night, so everyone on board endured a terrifying period of darkness while the ship rolled heavily and periodically struck the reef with violence. At daybreak the weather eased and the passengers were lowered over the stern in a wooden chair fixed to a rope, and then transferred by boat to a nearby islet. This was covered with weed and vermin, and there was no shelter. The crew salvaged some water and food, and made a tent from sails, but the 117 survivors could only tolerate this existence for a short time, especially as daytime temperatures rose to 44°C. John King must have known there was a high likelihood that they would die. The captain and some of the crew set out in an open boat to find help, and returned ten days later on a steamship that took everyone back to the UK.

On returning to England, John King's next ship was, unfortunately, SS *London*. There were other survivors of *Duncan Dunbar* on board *London*, but only John King lived through both incidents.

After the public hearing into the loss of the ship, it was reported that John King had lost everything in the wreck and had only 2 shillings to his name. Within days, a newspaper campaign helped to raise about £100 to support and reward him.

Portrait of John King.

42

Transported convict Thomas Berwick

Berwick instigated the wrecking of his own ship for profit, but was caught

Deliberately wrecking a ship to claim the insurance money probably occurred more commonly than was reported, but catching the perpetrators was difficult. They typically insured the ship for more than it was worth, and sometimes even stole valuable cargo and replaced it with worthless goods, and then employed someone on board to scuttle the ship.

In 1866 Thomas Berwick and Lionel Holdsworth bought a ship, *Severn*, and appointed Hugh Leyland as captain to sail from Newport to Shanghai. The owners supplied the ship's mate – a shady character called Charles Webb – who 'knew what he was sent on board for'. Berwick told Leyland it would cost £7,000 to put the ship to sea, but that they intended to insure it for between £8,000 and £9,000 and that they did not think it would reach China. If the ship sank, Captain Leyland would be paid £700, and he was advised to over-insure his personal possessions.

Severn put to sea, yet soon began taking on water. The ship's pumps coped initially, but off west Africa the influx became overwhelming. Leyland challenged Webb and he admitted drilling holes in the ship's hull. Webb also revealed that the boxes of cargo labelled as expensive firearms just contained salt.

The crew abandoned ship and *Severn* sank, Leyland destroying the ship's log. They were picked up by a passing ship and made their way back to England. Webb disclosed that some of the crew had seen his drill-holes and might make trouble but insisted he would 'talk them over or buy them over'. He confessed that he had drilled holes to sink another ship for Berwick,

Jane Brown. Once back in England, a false log was created and Leyland authenticated it.

At the trial, a garrulous Captain Leyland turned informer because he knew they'd been found out. He admitted to turning a blind eye and acting as accomplice. Nonetheless, he said his intention was to frustrate Webb's efforts, and that he'd had no idea how the scuttling was to be done.

Webb's attempts to silence the crew failed. None of them recognised the false log in terms of content or appearance. After abandoning ship, many had seen freshly drilled holes below the water line as the stricken vessel rose and fell. The ship's carpenter testified that Webb had prevented him searching the ship for leaks. The scandal was revealed in full and the verdict at the Old Bailey was a foregone conclusion. Webb was sentenced to ten years in prison, but Berwick and Holdsworth, as the instigators, were each given twenty years. Leyland was not tried.

Berwick and Holdsworth were transported to Australia on the same ship. When Berwick was eventually released, his humiliated wife and children refused to join him in Australia. This photo, with scribble marks all over his face, may have belonged to an ashamed family member.

43

Fragment of HMS Captain's bowsprit

One man's frustration, arrogance and wounded pride caused the deaths of nearly five hundred men

Captain Cowper Coles had a good idea. In 1855, during the Crimean War, he constructed a raft carrying a gun that could float close inshore, and he used it to bombard the Russian town of Taganrog. From this idea he came up with an even better one.

He designed a rotating metal dome or shield, beneath which a single gun could be made to point through all points of the compass. This gun turret enabled a vessel to fire shells in any direction without having to manoeuvre the ship. In the 1860s the Admiralty built vessels

The wilful Captain Cowper Coles.

with Coles' gun turrets for coastal defence, but remained hesitant about using the new design on ocean-going ships.

In the 1860s ships needed masts and sails, which inevitably got in the way of a rotating turret; solving this problem was complicated. Coles was allowed to begin two successive prototype ships, but in each case the Admiralty interfered, suspending one project and significantly modifying his designs for the other.

Coles became frustrated, and lobbied against his own employer so strongly that the Admiralty fired him. But that didn't stop Coles. He used his social connections to urge letters to the press and speeches in Parliament, winning over significant public opinion. The pressure was such that the Admiralty felt bound to rehire him and let him have his own way. The result was the building of HMS *Captain*.

Throughout its construction, the design of *Captain* was criticised by experienced and powerful figures, especially Robert Spencer Robinson, controller of the Navy, and others. They felt the ship was too heavy, sat too low in the water and its centre of gravity was too high. Coles ignored their objections, but his critics were to be proved correct.

After *Captain*'s launch in 1870, Coles seemed vindicated when its gunnery power was demonstrated. However, on 6 September *Captain* was cruising off Spain in heavy seas. Waves inundated the decks alarmingly, and as the wind increased to gale force the ship lurched, then simply rolled upside down and sank within a few minutes. Around 480 men drowned, including Coles; twenty-seven were picked up alive.

The subsequent court martial found it convenient to blame *Captain*'s constructors (even though Coles was meant to be supervising them) because they had departed from Coles' design. Yet the court also wished to place on record 'their conviction that the *Captain* was built in deference to public opinion, expressed in Parliament, and in opposition to the views and opinions of the Controller and his department, and that the evidence all tends to show that they generally disapproved of her construction'.

Undoubtedly, Coles was ahead of his time but his determination to build 'his ship his way' and prove his critics wrong – despite expert opinion to the contrary and inadequate sea trials – was the ultimate cause of this sad disaster. Part of *Captain*'s bowsprit, left floating after the ship sank, was used to make souvenirs for an eager public, such as the example shown on the previous page.

44

Sheet music and lyrics

A song commemorating the survival of a little girl from the notorious wreck of Northfleet *in 1873*

This song has the alternative title of 'Father Put Me in the Boat'. Its lyrics were written by William Gordon and the score was by Alfred Lee, best known for his arrangement of the song 'The Daring Young Man on the Flying Trapeze'. 'Wreck of the Northfleet' was composed to mark the infamous shipwreck off Dungeness, Kent, on 22 January 1873. The vessel was bound for Tasmania, taking labourers and their families to build a railway. There were 379 people on board. Whilst anchored at night in the English Channel during a storm, *Northfleet* was struck by a Spanish steamer, *Murillo*. The steamer did not stop to raise the alarm or help passengers, but simply fled. *Northfleet* started taking on water immediately; heavily laden as it was with iron railway lines and construction equipment, it sank within thirty minutes.

In the hasty confusion of launching the ship's boats in the darkness, *Northfleet*'s captain, Edward Knowles, grabbed his pistol and threatened to shoot any men who left the ship before the women and children could be evacuated. He even shot one man in the leg, but the other men ignored him and saved themselves. Only two women, a child and a baby were amongst the eighty-nine survivors.

The surviving child was 10-year-old Maria Taplin, who was placed in the lifeboat by her father, John, and the song is her unhappy story. The refrain has poor Maria crying: 'Oh father put me in the boat, Oh do not leave me here to die.'

John Taplin tried in vain to save his wife and other daughters, but the lifeboat left crammed with men who had fought for a place on board, and he had no chance. Poor Maria lost both her parents and two sisters that night. When the story of Maria's plight broke, women from all around the UK wrote and offered to adopt Maria, and the Queen herself asked for personal assurance that the child would be looked after. However, it was discovered that Maria had relatives living in Holloway and she went to stay with them.

The attitude of the crew of *Murillo*, who had abandoned hundreds of people to drown, provoked outrage. When the British authorities caught up with the vessel eight months later, it was impounded and sold to reimburse *Northfleet*'s owners for the loss of their ship. *Murillo*'s officers were severely criticised but as Spanish citizens were never brought to trial in the UK.

It seems odd, to modern tastes, to write a song about such a tragedy. The publication of songs as sheet music built on the traditional use of ballads to share news or advice or to tell a tale. Ballads were essentially song lyrics printed without a score and sold cheaply on the streets. Ballad sheets or 'broadsides' rarely survive, but are known to have been written about well-known nineteenth-century shipwrecks, including *Tayleur* (1854), SS *London* (1866), *Cospatrick* (1874) and *Indian Chief* (1881), amongst many others. This tradition continued into the early twentieth century, with its last major outing being for RMS *Titanic* in 1912, a disaster that spawned many songs and musical compositions.

Sadly, once the media interest died down poor Maria Taplin was sent by her relatives to an orphanage, where she died of tuberculosis just six years later.

CAPTAIN KNOWLES,
LOST IN THE NORTHFLEET OFF DUNGENESS, JAN. 22, 1873.
Stereoscopic Co.   *Copyright.*

Captain Knowles, who tried to enforce order with a firearm.

Maria Taplin.

45

Hand-drawn map of the coast of Chile

A dangerous part of the world as far as ships were concerned, but its politics were hazardous too

The coastline of South America has often proved treacherous to shipping, none more so than the coast of Chile. This map was drawn by a young officer, William Edwards, on board SS *Tacna* to help him learn the route to follow through the complex pattern of islands, headlands and bays of southern Chile. He worked for the Pacific Steam Navigation Company (PSNC), an organisation that had pioneered shipping routes from Europe to South America, as well as operating many local ships that carried mail, cargo and passengers.

Unfortunately, the 1870s were not a good decade for the Company: it was to lose six ships in the region. In 1871 SS *Iquique* sank, and in 1874 *Tacna* itself was wrecked. *Tacna* had been overladen at Valparaíso and began to list when the wind forced it to alter course. All efforts to correct the problem were in vain and the vessel turned over, exploded and sank half an hour later, drowning nineteen people. An eight-day court of inquiry under the British Consul to Chile found that overloading was the principal cause and the ship's captain, John Hyde, was principally at fault. He was formally reprimanded, although the port authorities took some share of the blame. It was not usual at this time for ship-owners or captains to be prosecuted for lives lost as a result of a wreck.

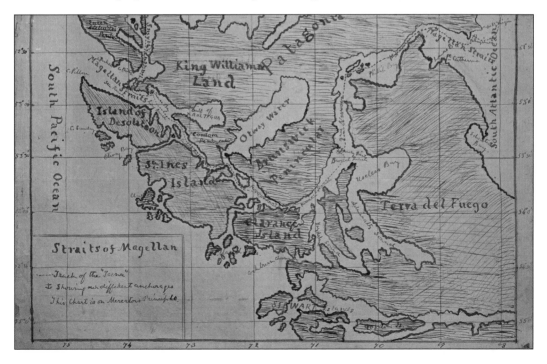

The deaths and the loss of the ship were tragic, but the ordeal was not yet over for Captain Hyde. Much to his surprise he was arrested by the Chilean government and thrown in prison to be subsequently tried for the loss of life caused. There was justifiable outrage in Chile that Hyde would 'go free', but additionally a certain amount of jealousy concerning the pre-eminence of a British company in their waters. Hyde's imprisonment rapidly escalated into a major diplomatic incident. Britain complained vociferously and despatched warships to the area to back up its insistence that Hyde be released and even compensated for wrongful arrest. British newspapers were filled with the story of the 'Tacna Affair' and all agreed that Chile would have no option but to back down, which eventually happened.

However, this was not the end of woes for PSNC, its ships and those travelling on them. In 1877 the Company lost three more ships: *Atacama*, *Valparaiso* and *Eten*, and in 1879 a fourth, *Illimani*. The steamships *Atacama* and *Eten* were sister ships and both ran aground off Chile within about four months, with the loss of around a hundred lives each. No one died on *Illimani*, but the circumstances surrounding the deaths of some of those aboard SS *Eten* were especially heartrending. About twenty people scrambled onto an isolated rock, but it was baking hot, there was no water and no one could reach them. In desperation, they flung themselves into the sea, hoping for a quick death. Although they had given up all hope, three of them managed to survive.

VALPARAISO, Saturday, May 2, 1874.

PACIFIC STEAM NAVIGATION COMPANY,

TIME TABLE
OF THE STEAMERS BETWEEN PANAMA, GUAYAQUIL, PAYTA, CALLAO, VALPARAISO, AND INTERMEDIATE PORTS.

COMMUNICATION FOUR TIMES PER MONTH WITH THE ISTHMUS OF PANAMÁ

The Company's fleet consists of the following magnificent steamers.

	Tonnage.	Horse-Power.		Tonnage.	Horse-Power.		Tonnage.	Horse-Power.
ACONCAGUA	3376	600	ETEN	1975	300	PATAGONIA	2784	500
ARAUCANIA	3085	590	GALICIA	3500	600	PAYTA	1806	400
AREQUIPA	1329	300	GARONNE	3088	500	PERU	1400	400
ATACAMA	1975	300	GUAYAQUIL	750	250	PERUANO	570	150
ATLAS	50	20	HUACHO	449	50	POTOSI	3500	600
AYACUCHO	7200	400	IBERIA			PUNO	3500	600
BAJA	100	20	ILLIMANI	3424	600	QUITO	800	250
BOGOTA	1600	400	ILO	1975	300	SAN CARLOS	750	270
BRITANNIA	3500	600	INCA	296	80	SANTA ROSA	2000	400
CALDERA	1740	350	IQUIQUE	450	50	SANTIAGO	1500	250
CALLAO	1062	400	ISLAY	1500	300	SORATA	3423	600
CHILE	1750	450	JOHN ELDER	3088	500	SUPE	432	50
CHIMBORAZO	3088	500	LIMA	3200	500	TABOGUILLA	240	40
COLOMBIA	2300	500	LIMENA	2088	450	TALCA	700	200
COQUIMBO	1975	300	LUSITANIA	3088	500	TRUJILLO	1500	250
CORCOVADO	3500	600	MAGELLAN	2784	500	VALDIVIA	1975	300
CORDILLERA	2784	500	OROYA	1500	300	VALPARAISO	3423	600
COTAPAXI	3423	600	PACIFIC	2008	450			
CUZCO	3088		PANAMA	2008	450			

	SANTIAGO.		ISLAY.		OROYA.	
Leaves Panama	April 10		April 16		April 25	
Arrives at Guayaquil			19		29	
Do Payta	14		21		May 1	
Do Callao	16		23			

	LIMA.	AYACUCHO.	COLOMBIA.	COQUIMBO.	PANAMA.	ATACAMA.
Leaves Callao	April 18	April 22	April 25	April 29	May 2	May 6
Arrives at Tambo de Mora	19	23	26	30	3	7
Do Pisco	19	23	26	30	3	7
Do Lomas			24	May 1		8
Do Chala	20			27	4	
Do Quilca					2	
Do Islay	21	25	28	2	5	9
Do Mollendo	21	25	28	2	5	9
Do Ilo	21		28		5	
Do Arica	22	26	29	3	6	10
Do Pisagua	23	27	30	4	7	11
Do Mejillones		27	30	4	7	11
Do Iquique	23	27	30	4	7	11
Do Tocopilla	24		May 1		8	
Do Cobija	24	28	1	5	8	12
Do Mejillones (Bol.)	24		1		8	
Do Antofagasta	25	28	2	5	9	12
Do Chañaral	26	29	3	6	10	13
Do Caldera	26	29	3	6	10	13
Do Carrizal Bajo	27		3		11	
Do Huasco	27		4		11	
Do Coquimbo	27	30	4	7	12	14
Do Valparaiso	29	May 1	6	8	13	15

PSNC had a huge fleet of ships and dominated the South American market.

46

Sketch of survivors

The only people to live through the frightening destruction and wreck of Cospatrick

This sketch by an unknown artist shows three people from the ill-fated *Cospatrick*. From left to right they are Edward Cotter, ordinary seaman; Henry MacDonald, second mate; and Thomas Lewis, quartermaster. They were the only survivors from one of the nineteenth century's most appalling disasters at sea. The ship had carried over 470 people.

Cospatrick was an emigrant ship, bound for Auckland, New Zealand. It departed Gravesend on 11 September 1874 with approximately 429 emigrants on board, and a crew of about forty-four. At midnight on 17 November everyone was awoken by cries of 'Fire!' It was a dread warning and it had to be dealt with speedily. The ship was in the middle of the ocean, several hundred miles southwest of Cape Town, with no hope of assistance.

The crew tried desperately to put out the fire but to no avail, and the wind fanned the flames, making it worse; *Cospatrick* was also carrying

much inflammable cargo such as kerosene, coal and spirits. The fire raced out of control and the passengers understandably panicked.

The boats would hold fewer than half the people on board but the first ones to be launched, carrying mostly women, were upset and tipped everyone into the sea. Two lifeboats did stay afloat – one holding thirty-two people was commanded by the chief mate, Charles Romaine, and the other, with thirty survivors, was under second mate Henry MacDonald.

The remainder of the people on board were faced with a stark choice: being burned alive or drowning. The ship's captain, Alexander Elmslie, made the grim decision for his family and threw his wife and 4-year-old son overboard before jumping himself to a certain death.

Unfortunately, the survivors' ordeal was only just beginning. A storm separated the two boats and Romaine's boat was never seen again. Meanwhile, although they saw out the storm, MacDonald's boat drifted for days. In their hasty departure there had been no time to grab any provisions, so they had no food or water; equally importantly, there was no mast and only one oar.

Everyone became progressively weaker, and then one by one they died, some becoming delirious in their final hours. It is horrible to learn that the survivors sucked blood from the corpses and ate their livers. After ten days adrift, on 27 November the boat was spotted by a ship, *British Sceptre*. Only five people were left alive, but they were weak and feeble and two of them died shortly afterwards. The crewmen MacDonald, Lewis and Cotter were the only ones to survive; all the emigrants died, even though there had been twenty-three in the boat originally.

The official inquiry concluded that the fire was probably caused by someone using a naked flame while attempting to steal items such as spirits in the darkness of the forward hold.

Cospatrick.

47

Plimsoll line

A practical method to prevent ship losses due to overloading

This representation of a ship's loading line appears at the base of a statue on Victoria Embankment, London. It was erected by the National Union of Seamen to commemorate the life and works of Samuel Plimsoll, MP for Derby.

Plimsoll and ship-owner James Hall were appalled by the hundreds of vessels wrecked every year, many of the losses were avoidable and a consequence of rapacious ship-owners who cared more for profits than they did for their crews. The term 'coffin ships' was coined for vessels in a poor state of repair that were sent to sea overloaded and over-insured. Clever manipulation of insurance meant that an owner could still make a profit whether their ship arrived safely with its cargo intact or sank on the way. It was a win-win for unscrupulous ship-

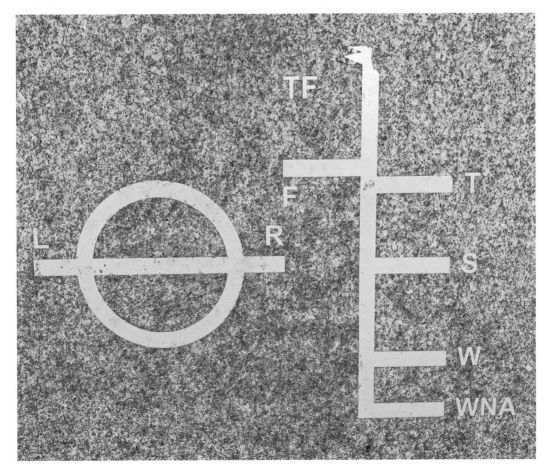

Plimsoll's laudatory medal.

owners, but caused the deaths of many poorly paid seamen and impoverished emigrants. All safety reforms of any kind were strongly resisted by the powerful ship-owners' lobby, who did not want to pay for them.

Plimsoll and Hall advocated that a line should be marked on all ships to show the maximum depth it could sink to in the water when loaded. Initially frustrated in his attempts, Plimsoll exposed the fact that a large number of MPs were ship-owners or in the pocket of shipping companies.

The matter was due to be debated in the House of Commons on 22 July 1875, but it was announced on the day that there would be no time for it. An angry Plimsoll leapt to his feet, shouting at MPs, shaking his fist, calling them 'villains' and refusing to be silenced. Shocked by this unparliamentary language, the Speaker asked him to retract his remarks, but Plimsoll refused and left the chamber. The fact that Plimsoll was so passionate about the subject earned him a great deal of respect, and a 'laudatory medal' was minted by his supporters to commemorate his taking MPs to task so publicly. On one side of the medal is a bust of Plimsoll; on the other, a sinking coffin ship with a skull on its sails.

Initial satisfaction amongst MPs that they had contrived to rebuff Plimsoll soon evaporated

because the public sided with their detractor. Plimsoll had cleverly prepared a detailed briefing for the newspapers outlining his arguments and they published them. Ministers were so concerned by the public outrage that they hastily invoked legislation along the lines that Plimsoll demanded. The Merchant Shipping Act of 1876 was not perfect, not least because it was ship-owners who decided where the 'Plimsoll line' was to be marked. However, crucially, the tide had turned somewhat in favour of safety over profit. Ship-owners were powerful men and forcing them to accept change was never going to be easy. It was only in the 1890s that the position of the loading line was standardised and no longer determined by the owner.

Samuel Plimsoll.

48

Anchor of HMS Eurydice

Remnant of a ship which mysteriously sank in 1878,
but which is still said to haunt the area

In 1878 the Royal Navy's cutting-edge ships had steel hulls and were powered by steam engines. In this respect the 35-year-old *Eurydice* was a vessel from a former era – a ship with a wooden hull and powered by sails. However, the navy clung tenaciously to the belief that its servicemen needed to understand how to work a sailing ship, despite the fact that such vessels were clearly obsolete. *Eurydice* had been a top-of-the-range frigate in its heyday and was kept going to train young recruits.

In spring 1878 it was heading back home to Portsmouth from Bermuda. On 22 March, off the Isle of Wight, *Eurydice* was charging ahead in a strong wind under full sail when it was suddenly engulfed in an intense snowstorm that seemed to come from nowhere. For reasons never satisfactorily explained, the ship unexpectedly toppled over and began sinking. There were only two survivors to tell the tale. Teenager Sydney Fletcher rushed up on deck and leapt overboard clutching a lifebuoy when he heard the order 'All

hands for themselves.' Barely had he entered the water than the ship sank, drawing him down beneath the icy waves, but the lifebuoy raised him up again. The other survivor, Benjamin Cuddiford, was a first-rate swimmer and many of his drowning messmates called out to him for help. Initially, he tried to aid them but with four men clinging to him, he was obliged to kick them off in order to save himself.

One of the youngest witnesses of the events was Winston Churchill who, as a child, saw the ship disappear into the storm from the clifftops while on holiday. Next day he saw the stubby masts protruding from the sea. It made a deep impression on him as a young boy because he later watched some of the bodies being brought ashore.

An attempt was made to salvage the ship but such was the macabre public interest that the remains had to be guarded by Royal Marines to prevent people pilfering keepsakes. It was eventually deemed unsuitable for salvage, but *Eurydice*'s anchor was retained and now forms part of a memorial to the victims at the Royal Navy Cemetery in Portsmouth. It remains one of the worst peacetime naval disasters, and the memorial identifies 362 men and boys who died.

Yet the story does not end there. Ever since its tragic loss, there have been persistent reports of a ghost ship which appears suddenly off the Isle of Wight near where *Eurydice* sank, and then abruptly disappears again. Perhaps the most dramatic encounter involved a 1930s submarine, whose commander had to alter course to avoid hitting a large sailing vessel, only to find the ship had vanished. In 1998 Prince Edward and a film crew reported seeing it when filming a documentary.

Whatever the truth of the matter, the Royal Navy has ever since avoided the unlucky name *Eurydice* for a vessel, despite repeatedly reusing many other ship names.

A ghostly ship in the fog off the Isle of Wight, but is it *Eurydice?*.

49

A silver sixpence

A sixpence to honour the victims of an infamous tragedy on the Thames

An autumnal cruise on the river Thames was a rare luxury in the lives of working Londoners and their families, who seldom had leisure time and had little money to spend. On 3 September 1878, for a fare of around 2 shillings, the paddle-steamer *Princess Alice* had taken passengers from the heart of London to the Kent coast for the day. In the later afternoon the small but crowded ferry began its return journey. The facilities on board included food and a band, and some passengers had personal cabins for the day.

At around 7.30pm *Princess Alice* rounded Tripcock Point near Woolwich, to be almost immediately confronted by a larger vessel, SS *Bywell Castle*, which was heading straight towards it. There was little time to react in the fading light. *Bywell Castle* smashed into the side of *Princess Alice*, damaging it so severely that the ship broke in two. There were screams and panic. Many passengers and crew were trapped below deck and had no chance to escape as the small ferry rapidly filled with water. Others were thrown into the river or leapt overboard, but this was an era when many people could not swim and Victorian clothes were bulky. The scene of the collision was also a section of the Thames that stank from all the sewage that poured into it. Frightened adults and children thrashed around in the putrid water trying to stay afloat, grabbing on to each other and anything that might float.

Bywell Castle escaped significant damage, and the crew threw down ropes, lifebuoys and other buoyant materials, and lowered its boats. Figures for the dead are uncertain. About 130 individuals were saved initially but some of them

later died, perhaps from swallowing sewage. At the time it was estimated that approximately 650 people died in the disaster. It took a long time to retrieve all the bodies.

Two legal processes took place in the wake of the tragedy, but arrived at different conclusions. A coroner's inquest determined that both vessels were at fault because neither had reacted appropriately. Conversely, a Board of Trade inquiry placed the blame firmly on *Princess Alice*, because it had contravened regulations stipulating that vessels approaching head-on from opposite directions should pass each other port to port. William Grinstead, master of *Princess Alice*, was deemed to have turned the wrong way and made collision inevitable. However, this conclusion is open to doubt since Grinstead died in the wreck and witnesses could not agree about what they had seen.

Around twenty-three thousand people contributed to ensure a memorial to the victims was established at Woolwich. This 'sixpenny fund' ensured that even the poorest families could make a contribution, such as the coin shown on the previous page, to honour family and friends lost.

Bywell Castle slamming into the crowded *Princess Alice* at dusk.

50

A captain's trunk

*Carried the possessions of a cowardly ship's master responsible
for 'the wreck that never was'*

This trunk accompanied Captain Joseph Lucas Clark during his career, a man notorious for an incident that was to make him well-known for all the wrong reasons.

In July 1880 Captain Clark was master of SS *Jeddah* taking 953 adult Muslim passengers from Penang to Saudi Arabia on a holy pilgrimage or Hajj, together with large numbers of children who were not enumerated. The ship's crew numbered fifty, and Captain Clark had also exercised the master's prerogative to share his quarters with his wife.

Jeddah experienced heavy weather for most of the voyage. By 3 August the wind had increased to almost hurricane force and the constant buffeting caused the ship's boilers to work loose from their fastenings. This does not seem to have concerned the ship's engineer as much as it should: he simply stuck a few wedges under the loose structure to restrict the movement. The weather worsened over the next three days, causing the feed valve to the port-side boiler to break. The ship had to be stopped for repairs while large waves crashed over it.

Jeddah was by now filling with water, and almost no sooner had the vessel got under way again than the constant shaking of the engines broke the starboard boiler. Repairs were ineffective and the ship continued under only one engine. All hands and the passengers were enlisted to

SHIPWRECKS IN 100 OBJECTS

work the pumps and to bail out using buckets. Despite their efforts, there was soon so much water in the engine room that it washed away the wedges supporting the engine, which shook itself to pieces, and extinguished the ship's fires. The engine was now useless, so sails were resorted to.

Captain Clark at no point communicated with the passengers or attempted to reassure them, despite land being only a few miles distant. Instead, incredibly enough, Captain Clark with his wife and some senior officers decided *Jeddah* was bound to founder and boarded a lifeboat to escape. Seeing this, the passengers attempted to storm the boat but the first officer produced a pistol and fired at them, enabling the officers to cut themselves free. In the ensuing mayhem aboard *Jeddah*, other crewmen attempted to flee, but they clashed with passengers, resulting in the deaths of twenty-one people, including the second mate.

After a few hours Clark's boat was picked up by SS *Scindia*, but the captain made no attempt to initiate a search for his stricken ship. Instead, he falsely reported that some officers had been murdered by the passengers and that he had witnessed *Jeddah* sinking with the loss of all on board.

It was to some amazement, therefore, that three days later SS *Jeddah* was towed into port by SS *Antenor*, which had found the ship drifting but in no immediate danger of sinking.

A court of inquiry at Aden found Clark guilty of gross misconduct, and indirectly responsible for the deaths of twenty-one people. The court dismissed as baseless Clark's excuse that their lives had been in danger from angry passengers. He was labelled a liar, a coward, incompetent, unprofessional and inhuman. Nonetheless his only punishment was to have his master's certificate taken away for three years, meaning he could not be a captain for this time.

Perhaps unsurprisingly, given the slack standards of accountability that then prevailed, this did not stop Clark continuing to go to sea. Indeed, this whole shameful episode might have fallen into complete obscurity were it not for the fact that author Joseph Conrad, himself a former merchant seaman, used these events as the basis for a popular novel. Published in 1900, *Lord Jim* tells the tale of a ship's mate who becomes ashamed that he joined his captain in abandoning 800 Muslims aboard the sinking SS *Patna*, only for it to be towed into port a few days later. Jim and his captain are censured at the court of inquiry, and the rest of the novel is concerned with Jim's guilt and his attempts at redemption.

51

Photo of Abraham Hart Youngs

He was still saving lives at sea when he was nearly 80

In the history of shipwrecks there have been many great acts of bravery. Notable amongst these are many lifeboatmen, such as Henry Blogg, Charles Fish and James Haylett. However, there are countless others who are now forgotten, especially amongst the coastguard, who have long had a vital role in saving lives at sea. Abraham Hart Youngs was a boatman for

the Sussex coastguard and an excellent swimmer. He was a tough character and did not shy away from action: arresting smugglers, for example, even when threatened with physical violence. During his long career he is credited with helping to save 170 lives on the coast of Britain, and was awarded four medals from the RNLI and the Royal Humane Society (RHS), as well as other honours.

There are too many incidents to record them all here, but in 1843 Youngs and others attended the wreck of *Prince Regent* near Brighton. The vessel was being driven onshore in a storm and the crew were trapped. The gallant conduct of Youngs was very conspicuous, as he waded and then swam through the heavy surf and breaking waves to get a line to the crewmen. He also had to contend with the 'malevolent efforts of some fishermen to detain him, and throw him down'. He, however, succeeded in getting the lifeline home and the crew were all landed safely. He received an RHS silver medal for this act of courage.

Five years later, in 1848, Youngs took part in a most difficult rescue off Newhaven. It was an extremely dark night with a very heavy sea, and the coastguard had been alerted that the Swedish schooner *Lafayette* was trapped in breaking waves off the shore. Again, Youngs volunteered to get to the wreck and ran out to it alone, despite the atrocious conditions. He was able to grab hold of part of the ship and reach the men, but in the process was seriously injured. Nonetheless, he still managed to get a line back to his colleagues on the beach. This enabled five men to be saved, although two others died. The conditions were so treacherous that Youngs nearly drowned and for a while his colleagues thought him lost; he survived, yet suffered badly from exposure afterwards. His bravery earned him an RNLI silver medal.

This photograph was taken in 1881 and shows the medals that Abraham had earned during his life. On the easel can be seen his latest award – a large testimonial for bravery from the Royal Humane Society. This final honour was given two years prior to the photograph when, aged a remarkable 79, he dived fully clothed from an open boat to save a drowning man. He didn't retire completely until he was 83.

52

Ship portrait as carte de visite

Magdala *was one of countless vessels that disappeared at sea*

A carte de visite was a pocket-sized image, in this case depicting a ship. It enabled a proud ship-owner or captain to carry around a likeness of their vessel to show to prospective customers. *Magdala* was a small barque of around 400 tons built in Sunderland in 1868. In 1882 it set sail from Cardiff for Indonesia under its captain Peter Nelson, carrying a cargo of coal and with a crew of ten men from five different nations. The ship was never seen again.

There are no official figures for vessels lost without trace in the nineteenth century, but it was alarmingly common. The most dramatic example was SS *City of Glasgow*, which left Liverpool for Philadelphia on 1 March 1854 with 480 people on board. It simply vanished somewhere in the Atlantic. To this day no one knows what happened to the ship, the crew or its passengers. The wreck has never been found, and it is the largest loss of life from any British ship that has disappeared.

The White Star Line's SS *Naronic* was a freighter that vanished in 1893 en route to New York with seventy-four people on board. Two empty lifeboats were found but its fate remains a mystery.

With all of these disasters, one wonders at the awful despair faced by relatives, who for months afterwards must have hoped that their loved ones had been washed up on a desert island or rescued by a passing ship that had been delayed reaching the UK. The 'not knowing' must have been agonising. Eighteen-year-old Percy Edwards joined SS *Bay of Cadiz* in 1888. When the ship was reported missing in 1889, his parents and the families of other crewmembers had to endure rumours that lights seen on a remote island might be castaways from the wreck. But when the island could eventually be reached there was no one there.

Although those who once grieved for the crew of *Magdala* are themselves long-since deceased, there might, at long last, be closure for the ship's story. In 2015 Australian experts searching the oceans for missing Malaysia Airlines flight MH370 found two Victorian shipwrecks 1,440 miles southwest of Australia. One was a wooden sailing vessel that seemed to have burst apart and was surrounded by coal. Analysis of the coal supported a UK origin, and records of missing ships suggested that the closest fit in terms of size was *Magdala*. Densely packed coal in a ship's hold could unexpectedly explode due to accumulation of methane gas or it could spontaneously combust in high temperatures. This may have been the sudden, frightening and lonely fate for the crew of *Magdala* in 1882.

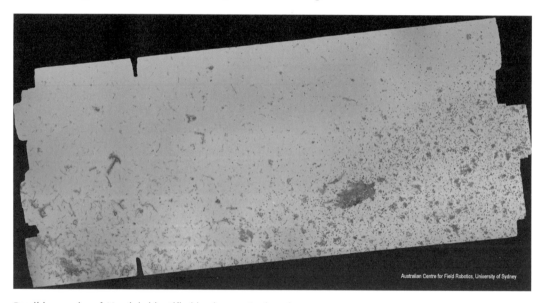

Australian Centre for Field Robotics, University of Sydney

Possible remains of *Magdala* identified by deep water imaging.

53

Memorial to Richard Parker

A man who was killed and eaten by his three starving crewmates after their vessel sank

Mignonette was a British yacht that had been purchased by an Australian. In 1884 four men were chosen to sail the vessel to its new owner: Tom Dudley was the skipper, Ted Brooks and Edwin Stephens were sailors, and 17-year-old Richard Parker was the cabin boy.

On 19 May 1884 the yacht departed Southampton and headed for Australia. All went well until 5 July, when suddenly the yacht was sunk by a huge wave somewhere between Madeira and Cape Town. Fortuitously, all four men leapt into a dinghy as *Mignonette* disappeared beneath the sea. Yet now they were alone and exposed in an open boat in the South Atlantic and the only provisions they had were two tins of turnips. There was no water. They managed to catch a turtle to eat, and garnered some meagre water supplies when it rained; they even drank their own urine. But it was not enough and they knew they would soon die of thirst if help did not arrive.

The inexperienced Richard Parker decided to drink large amounts of seawater to try to quench his thirst. This made him extremely ill, and soon

he was semi-conscious. His crewmates decided that their only hope of survival was to kill and eat Parker. After some hesitation, Stephens held down the weakened teenager while Dudley cut his throat. The three men drank his blood and then butchered the corpse, before throwing the carcass overboard. They survived on their gruesome store of human meat for several days, but eventually it ran out. However, it kept them alive and after twenty-four days afloat they were spotted by the German ship *Moctezuma* and within a month or so were back home.

Here, a new ordeal began for the survivors, who made no secret of what they had done. At the time it was widely supposed that the 'custom of the sea' permitted the murder of another person if that would allow other shipwreck victims to live – usually by drawing lots to select someone. It was a tragic necessity and assumed not to be illegal, largely because of established precedent. Only ten years previously, for example, some survivors of *Euxine* had murdered a crewmate and eaten him, and were allowed to go free.

In the case of *Mignonette*'s survivors, the authorities took a different view and the three men were prosecuted, to their complete astonishment. Interestingly, public sympathy was largely in support of the perpetrators. Brooks was exonerated by a local magistrate as he had not taken part in the killing, but the two others were referred to a higher court facing charges of murder. They were both convicted, which meant a death sentence, but they expected to be pardoned. In the end their sentence was commuted to six months in prison. However, this case set an important precedent: that 'necessity' was not a valid defence for murder at sea or anywhere else.

The *Mignonette* case also partly inspired Yann Martel, the author of philosophical novel *Life of Pi*. In this celebrated book, a tiger, an Indian boy and others survive a shipwreck and the author chose to name the big cat Richard Parker. The story refers to cannibalism but, in a reversal of his real-life role, the character of Richard Parker is not a victim.

First innings cricket scores

After playing Shanghai, most of the Hong Kong cricket team were lost in a maritime tragedy

Shanghai and Hong Kong first played each other at cricket in the 1860s. The two teams were comprised of British men stationed in each city, many of them in the military. In 1892 Hong Kong had beaten Shanghai at home, and in October the team travelled to Shanghai for the return fixture, which their opponents won convincingly.

Although defeated, Hong Kong's bowler James Lowson was pleased with his performance in the first innings, taking eight wickets. The cricketers boarded the P&O steamer *Bokhara* to sail home on 8 October. Ominously, the ship ran into a fearsome typhoon on 10 October. The captain struggled to keep the ship at sea, but it was driven landwards and the conditions became so severe that all the ship's boats were destroyed. At 10pm enormous waves washed over the ship and put out the engine room fires. Shortly afterwards, rocks were spotted to the lee side. The ship's officers calmly shook hands: they knew there was nothing they could do without a functioning engine.

In the darkness *Bokhara* struck rocks surrounding the Penghu Islands off the coast of modern Taiwan. The ship sank quickly and most people were drowned. However, at the last minute, incredible though it may seem, a large wave lifted twenty-three people off the deck and threw them to safety on the adjacent Sand Island. The survivors included two of the Hong Kong cricketers, Lowson and Lieutenant Markham.

```
Shanghai vs. Hong Kong Interport Match
Shanghai Cricket Club Ground, Shanghai
3rd - 4th October 1892
SHANGHAI WON BY 157 RUNS

Shanghai First Innings
W.A.H. Moule        b.Lowson              2
A.P. Wood           c.Dawson b.Lowson    25
F.J. Abbott         b.Lowson             16
P. Wallace          b.Lowson              4
A.J.H. Moule        c.Donegan b.Lowson   10
C.S. Barff          c.Jeffkins b.Lowson   0
J. Mann             b.Lowson              7
W. Bruce-Rob'son    b.Mumford            11
D.W. Crawford       b.Lowson              2
A.G.H. Carruthers   not out              30
A.P. Nichol         c.Lowson b.Donegan    0

Extras                                    0
Total (all out)    (76 overs)           112
```

Hong Kong Bowling

	O	M	R	W	Wd	NB
J.A. Lowson	37	19	66	8	0	0
T.W. Donegan	21	8	25	1	0	0
G. Mumford	18	11	18	1	0	0

```
Hong Kong First Innings
J.A. Lowson         b.Barff              10
F.G. Jeffkins       b.Carruthers         13
J. Dunn             b.Carruthers         16
T.W. Donegan        b.Carruthers          0
F.D. Markham        c.Abbott b.Barff      6
C.G. Boyle          c.Mann b.Barff        5
R.H. Dawson         c.Moule b.Nichol      7
G.E. Taverner       b.Carruthers          7
C. Wallace          lbw.Carruthers        9
F.A. Burnett        b.Barff               0
G. Mumford          not out               0

Extras             (5 lb)                 5
Total (all out)    (43.0 overs)          78
```

Shanghai Bowling

	O	M	R	W	Wd	NB
C.S. Barff	19	7	33	4	0	0
A.G.H. Carruthers	21	7	29	5	0	0
A.P. Nichol	3	3	11	1	0	0

On the island the survivors found a deserted hut and managed to subsist there, hoping that they might be rescued. Two days after the wreck, some local fishermen came in sight, heavily armed, intending to scour the area for wreckage. Lowson later recalled, 'At first we apprehended murderous intentions on their part, but the chief officer rigged up a flag and I went to parley with them. I succeeded in inducing them to take us all to the village of Peho, where we were very well treated.' They were summoned to the town of Makung (modern Magong) to meet the area's local governor or Chuntai. It was a long and wearisome tramp of 5 miles or so in the heat.

Yet when they arrived, Lowson wrote, 'it is impossible to imagine a better reception'. They were fed and cared for with great kindness.

They were eventually transported back to Hong Kong by HMS *Porpoise*, but the citizens of Hong Kong were so impressed by the Chuntai's care of the shipwreck victims that a collection was held in gratitude. He was invited on board HMS *Porpoise* as guest of honour, where a sum of money and an engraved silver plate were presented to him.

Hong Kong and Shanghai still play each other at cricket and when they do, the victor receives the Bokhara Bell Memorial Trophy in remembrance of the sad events of 1892.

Photo of the two teams. James Lowson is the central figure in a chair, and Markham is seated on the ground to his right.

55

Advert for a lecture

James Curran survived the bizarre sinking of HMS Victoria *and gave talks about it*

HMS *Victoria* was a powerful, cutting-edge vessel, the flagship of Vice Admiral Sir George Tryon, who commanded the Royal Navy's Mediterranean fleet. On 22 June 1893, while on manoeuvres off Lebanon, Tryon split his fleet into two parallel columns. One was led by Tryon in *Victoria*, the other by Rear Admiral Albert Markham in HMS *Camperdown*. Inexplicably, Tryon ordered the two leading ships in each column to turn towards each other, even though there was clearly inadequate space for such a manoeuvre. Tryon's own senior officers knew this, yet the rigid discipline of the Royal Navy made querying his orders simply impossible. Markham dared to hesitate and Tryon signalled to him: 'What are you waiting for?'

The manoeuvre took place as ordered and the almost inevitable collision occurred. *Camperdown* sliced a huge hole in *Victoria*'s starboard side. There was insufficient time to close its watertight doors, and the sea gushed in. *Victoria* sank in just thirteen minutes. It all happened too quickly to launch any lifeboats and around 360 men drowned, including Tryon. Many were trapped on board the sinking ship or, despite being in the water, were dragged down by suction as *Victoria* foundered. Some poor souls were sliced apart by the still-rotating propellers. However, some three hundred or more survived, picked up by boats from the other ships of the fleet.

A court martial found Tryon entirely to blame for the tragedy. Witnesses had heard him exclaim that it was all his fault shortly before the ship went down.

Meanwhile, James Curran, a 20-year-old stoker who survived *Victoria*'s sinking, recognised an opportunity to make a new career. He left the navy and gave public talks about his experience. He was soon employed by Joseph Poole's Myriorama show, which

JAMES CURRAN,
A Survivor of H.M.S. VICTORIA who relates his personal experiences at each representation of
JOSEPH POOLE'S MYRIORAMA.

R. Dighton's Art Studio CHELTENHAM

enlisted Curran to talk about the loss of HMS *Victoria* while his colleagues rotated large coloured canvasses, and deployed lights, sound effects, music and moving models of the ships. This travelling 'sound and light' show performed at venues all around the UK, being advertised in newspapers and via cards such as the one shown on the previous page. It was popular with audiences, and Curran wrote that his career as a performer earned him four times as much as his naval wages.

There was another notable survivor of the sinking of HMS *Victoria*: a young officer named John Jellicoe. He was later to find fame commanding the British Grand Fleet at the Battle of Jutland in the First World War.

A Victorian lantern slide showing *Victoria*'s fate.

56

Chalice

One of many gifts recognising the compassion of rescuers after SS Drummond Castle *sank in 1896*

SS *Drummond Castle* departed Cape Town on 28 May 1896, bound for London. One day from its final destination, on 16 June, the ship should have sailed to the north of Ushant, an island off Brittany at the southwestern end of the English Channel. Yet for some inexplicable reason the vessel's captain went south of the island, where there are many rocks. The sea was calm but foggy, and it was night-time, so poor visibility is the only excuse for this strange decision.

Charles Marquardt was a passenger on board. He was in the smoking room at about 10.30pm when he felt a slight concussion, no more than might be felt when a ship judders against a pier while docking. Someone said, 'That's a collision!' Charles ran on deck and saw the ship was sinking, so raced to his cabin to get a lifebelt. He had never been shown how to wear it, but he tied it onto himself as best he could. To the great alarm of everyone on board, *Drummond Castle* sank in just four minutes and there was no time to launch any boats.

Before he knew it, Charles was in the water. 'Throughout the night,' he said, 'I clung to a floating spar, trying in vain to save exhausted fellow creatures from dropping off. After many weary hours I was rescued by a fisherman named Berthelet and taken to Ushant.'

Charles saw no other survivors, although there had been about 250 people on board. He sent a short telegram to the ship-owners, the Castle Line, in London: 'Drummond Castle total loss off Ushant. Am probably sole survivor.' In fact, two other people had survived – both sailors.

The British public were appalled, and when the news broke in South Africa the nation was stunned because 'barely a town had escaped without loss'.

The kindness and humanity of local people at the scene of the disaster met with universal praise. Not only had they rescued the few survivors, but they also retrieved many bodies and gave them a Christian burial. Queen Victoria was particularly touched and instructed that the rescuers and searchers be rewarded. A special silver medal was struck with the legend 'from Queen Victoria a token of gratitude' and issued to around 280 people.

The Archbishop of Canterbury was also moved, and sent the gilded chalice shown on the next page as a gift for the church on the island of Molène, where many of the rescuers lived. These islanders often struggled to find enough fresh water on their rocky outpost, so the British constructed a large cistern to collect and store rainwater, and donated a public clock so that fishermen could sail according to tide times. In addition, a church spire was built for the inhabitants of Ushant so that it could be used as a landmark by local fishermen. Much of this work was funded by donations from UK citizens.

57

Board of Trade wreck report

Government inquiries into wrecks were of little value for improving safety

The Board of Trade was the government department responsible for commercial shipping and safety at sea. It conducted inquiries into British ships lost at sea, especially where there was loss of life, aiming to learn lessons from disasters and to hold accountable those at fault. At least, that was the theory.

In practice, the inquiries were thorough but of limited impact, especially in the nineteenth century. The Board of Trade's recommendations were seldom translated into laws. The government pandered to wealthy ship-owners who were rarely criticised, and never penalised financially or prosecuted even when at fault. In Victorian society it was also considered improper to criticise a ship's captain if he died as a result of a shipwreck, even if he was to blame. Captains were 'gentlemen' and going down with your ship was the right thing to do, and was penalty enough if you made a mistake.

The inquiry shown here is for the loss of SS *Mohegan*. At 6.50pm on 14 October 1898 *Mohegan* ploughed onto rocks off the Lizard, Cornwall, tearing out the ship's bottom. It foundered quickly. Local lifeboats saved some people, but only one of *Mohegan*'s boats was launched. More than a hundred people died, and fifty-one were saved.

(No. 5803.)

"MOHEGAN" (S.S.).

The Merchant Shipping Act, 1894.

In the matter of a formal investigation held at the Guildhall, Westminster, on the 10th and 11th, 24th and 25th, and at the Town Hall, Westminster, on the 12th and 26th days of November, 1898, before R. H. B. Marsham, Esq., assisted by Captain Ronaldson, Mr. Hallett, C.E., and Captain Dyer, R.N., into the circumstances attending the stranding and total loss of the British s.s. "Mohegan," on the Manacle Rocks, near the Lizard, on the 14th of October last, whereby loss of life ensued.

Report of Court.

The Court having carefully inquired into the circumstances attending the above-mentioned shipping casualty, finds for the reasons stated in the Annex hereto, that the cause of the stranding of the vessel was, in their opinion, that a wrong course—W. by N.—was steered after passing the Eddystone, at 4.17 p.m., on the 14th October last, and that the deplorable loss of so many lives was in consequence of the vessel taking a very sudden and serious list to port, of her going down in not more than a quarter of an hour from the time of striking, and of there being no light to indicate her position through the electric light having gone out.

Dated this 30th day of November, 1898.

R. H. B. Marsham, Judge.

We concur in the above report.

A. Ronaldson,
J. H. Hallett, C.E.,
Richd. C. Dyer,
} Assessors.

Annex to the Report.

This inquiry was held at the Guildhall, Westminster, on the 10th and 11th November, at the Town Hall, Westminster, on the 12th November, at the Guildhall, Westminster, on the 24th and 25th November, and was concluded at the Town Hall, Westminster, on the 26th November, 1898.

Mr. H. R. Massel Jones, with whom was Mr. Butler Aspinall, appeared on behalf of the Board of Trade; Mr. Pyke, with whom was Mr. Arthur Pritchard, represented the owners of the "Mohegan," the Atlantic Transport Company, Limited, and the representatives of the officers not represented by Mr. Nelson; Mr. Nelson appeared on behalf of the representatives of the master and third officer of the vessel; whilst Mr. Charles Cunninghame Graham, of the Royal National Lifeboat Institution, represented it.

The "Mohegan," late "Cleopatra," official number 109,043, was a steel screw steamship, built by Messrs. Earle's Shipbuilding and Engineering Company, Limited, at Hull, for Messrs. Thomas Wilson & Company, Limited, of Hull, but before she was launched she was purchased by the Atlantic Transport Steamship Company, Limited, of London, on the 22nd July, 1898, along with some other vessels from Messrs. Wilson & Leyland, with the goodwill of their New York trade; Mr. Alfred Strover Williams, of 108, Fenchurch Street, London, E.C., being the designated manager, and she was registered at the port of Hull.

Her dimensions were: length, 482·4 ft.; breadth, 52·1 ft.; depth from top of beam amidships to top of keel, 35·7 ft. She had four steel masts. She was fitted with triple expansion vertical direct acting engines, built by Messrs. Earle's Shipbuilding and Engineering Company, Limited; she had three cylinders of the following dimensions: 32 ins., 54 ins., and 90 ins., with a stroke of 66 ins. She had four boilers, built of steel, which were loaded with working pressure of 200 lbs. per square inch; with

1157—180—12/98 Wt 8 D & S 1

an indicated horse power of 5,50 , her speed would be 14 knots. She was lighted throughout by electricity; for this purpose she was fitted with duplicate sets of dynamos, each of which was compound wound, and were capable of an output of 300 amperes at 100 volts, the motive power being a double acting compound engine, built and supplied by Messrs. Belliss & Company, Limited, of Birmingham. Each of these dynamos were capable of lighting the whole of the ship's installation, in case of breakdown.

The wiring was on the latest double wire distributing box system. She was fitted with the usual steam pumps to the main engines, and also a large centrifugal circulating pump, together with an auxiliary duplex pump, and an ordinary pump of large size; these were fitted so that they could be connected to each compartment, and each compartment could be pumped out either by steam or hand.

She had two steel decks below her upper-deck, which was of pine, and eight water-tight bulkheads extending from keel to the upper-deck, only one of which was pierced, and that one was fitted with a water-tight door on an approved plan.

On the upper-deck she had a shelter-deck for cattle, above this deck was an enclosed bridge extending the whole length of the engine and boiler space, somewhat aft and forward of them. This contained the state-room and passengers' accommodation. Over the bridge-deck was a large steel house containing the music-room, saloon, smoking-room and state-rooms; the top was extended as a deck to the ship's side, and formed the boat-deck. She had eight boats, six being lifeboats, built of steel, of the aggregate capacity of 2,343 cubic feet, and capable of accommodating 234 persons; and wooden boats of the aggregate capacity of 472 cubic feet, and capable of accommodating 59 persons. They were carried on davits fitted with falls and patent disengaging gear, inboard on chocks. She had 250 lifebelts and 12 life-buoys. She was constructed under Lloyds' special survey, and was registered 100 A1.

She had three compasses on deck, one—Lord Kelvin's patent—on the flying bridge, by which the courses were set and steered, one in the wheel-house, underneath the bridge, and one aft. She was steered by steam. She had only made one voyage, to New York and back.

Mr. Charles Henry Wilson, M.P., of the firm of Wilson, Sons & Company, of Hull, stated that his firm had entered into a contract with Messrs. Earle & Company for the building of the "Cleopatra," afterwards called the "Mohegan," and four other steamers; that she was built under special survey, and that she and the four other vessels were being built for the passenger trade between London and New York. Mr. Wilson was the chairman of the Hull firm, and also of the London company of Messrs. Furness, Wilson & Leyland.

During the late war the American Government purchased steamers of the Atlantic Transport Company, and it was to replace these that the Company purchased the five steamers that were being built. For the "Cleopatra" they paid £140,000. She was insured for £112,000 at Lloyds' and other offices, the owners taking £28,000 on her themselves.

Mr. F. H. Pearson, assistant general manager of Earle's Shipbuilding Company, put in a statement including the specification of the vessel, and stated that when she was in dock at Hull before leaving, all the boats were lowered into the water in the presence of the Board of Trade officials, and that it took—employing eight men—about five minutes to lower and rehoist them. A rail was built on the boat-deck for the purpose of preventing passengers falling overboard.

The steamship "Mohegan" when completed left Hull on the 29th July, 1898, for London, she was then named the "Cleopatra," that being her launching name. It is worthy of notice that this steamer left the port of Hull without ballast or cargo; she arrived at Tilbury on the 30th July at about 11.30 a.m.

On this passage, through the negligence of one of the engineers, an accident happened to the boilers, the engineer on watch allowing the water to become too low in the port double-ended boiler; but, upon examination of the boiler in London, nothing was found wrong, and apparently no damage was done.

The inquiry's conclusions were that:

1. A wrong course was set which made it inevitable that *Mohegan* would hit the rocks. The captain saw the incorrect course and there were two other officers on the bridge as well.
2. The ship sank quickly and, due to flooding, all the electric lights went out within three minutes of the vessel striking rocks, so *Mohegan* could not be found easily at night by rescuers.

However, buried within the report are criticisms:

- The crew did not practise launching boats ('boat drill') on *Mohegan* before the disaster. Consequently, despite having fifteen minutes to launch the boats, only one got away. A passenger testified that boat drill did not occur on other ships owned by the same company. Even when boat drill happened, it took place in mid-ocean, but it ought to occur before sailing.

- Boats were not swung out ready to launch which delayed their deployment and cost lives. Some boats were of poor quality and broke apart before they could be used.
- The captain made a mistake with the ship's course 'inadvertently . . . and from over-confidence'. Nonetheless, officers or the look-out ought to have noticed that the ship was too close to land and raised the alert.
- *Mohegan* did not have easily accessible back-up lights or flares to show its position to rescuers at night. This delayed the rescue and cost lives.

Lessons about lifeboat inadequacy on passenger ships were repeatedly highlighted but disregarded throughout the nineteenth century. Wrecks were so common that they were regarded as almost inevitable and the result of 'bad luck', rather than the fault of negligent ship-owners or incompetent captains. About the best that inquiries could manage in practice was a reprimand for a culpable ship's captain or pilot if he survived the ordeal.

The remains of the *Mohegan* the day after its wreck.

58

Stained glass window

Liverpool Cathedral honours a woman who gave her life to save others in 1899

SS *Stella* plied the route between Southampton and the Channel Islands, and often took passengers on holiday. On 30 March 1899 it was carrying an uncertain number of passengers and crew perhaps totalling 220 or more. Amongst them was 46-year-old Mary Anne Rogers, the senior stewardess, who had served sixteen years at sea.

Unfortunately, a great disaster befell the ship, causing about 105 people to drown, as described succinctly in the *Illustrated London News*:

On Thursday afternoon, the day before Good Friday, in a thick fog between Alderney and Guernsey, the London and South-Western Railway Company's fine steamer *Stella*, which had left Southampton at a quarter past eleven in the forenoon, was caught among the Casquet rocks, on her way to the islands, and, going at high speed, her steel bottom was torn open in a few minutes on a submerged reef of sharp jagged stone; six boats, with many passengers, all the women and children, were quickly put afloat, and life-belts were supplied; but one large boat was capsized; the ship presently sank, rent asunder by the explosion of her steam-boilers as the sea poured into the engine-rooms; nearly all who had remained on board were drowned.

The ship sank very quickly but Mrs Rogers managed to save all the passengers under her charge. She calmed and reassured them, helped them into the boats, and insisted upon giving up her own lifebelt to a young woman who had become separated from her family.

As *Stella* began to go down, the sailors urged Mrs Rogers to escape but she refused; she realised that the lifeboat was already overloaded and her weight might capsize it. Instead she went down with the ship – the customary role for the captain, a man. By choosing to act as a professional member of the crew, Mrs Rogers earned instant national acclaim for her bravery.

The drinking fountain honouring Mrs Rogers in Southampton.

It struck a national chord: a large monumental drinking fountain honours her sacrifice on the waterfront at Southampton; there is a stained glass window bearing her image in Liverpool's Anglican Cathedral; and there is a plaque dedicated to her heroism in the City of London. Uniquely, the UK's three most important commercial ports at the time united to show their respect for an heroic individual.

Mrs Rogers left behind an elderly father and two children, dependent upon her. The British public responded quickly to a request for financial assistance, and £570 was raised – a big sum in 1899 – to ensure they were cared for. Some of this money paid for her memorial in Southampton, which says that her actions 'deserve perpetual commemoration because among the trivial pleasures and sordid strife of the world, they recall to us for ever the nobility and love-worthiness of human nature'.

Captain Reeks, who also went down with the ship, was subsequently strongly criticised in the official inquiry for not slowing down when he entered the fog.

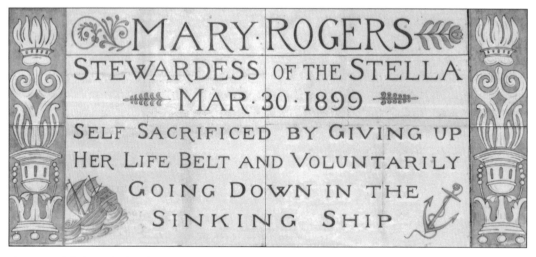

The memorial plaque in the City of London.

59

Maritime distress signals

*The ability for ships to call for urgent assistance was a
highly significant advance in safety*

Morse code was invented by Samuel Morse in the late 1830s, and significantly modified by Friedrich Gerke in 1848. It utilised a series of short and long electrical bursts tapped out manually – 'dots' and 'dashes' – to represent individual letters of the alphabet. These could be combined to send messages along a wire cable linking distant places using a telegraph system, first developed commercially by William Cooke and Charles Wheatstone.

The reliance on physical wires connecting locations meant that this useful method of communication could not be used aboard ships at sea. However, the pioneering work on radio by Guglielmo Marconi led to his development of what was called wireless telegraphy in which Morse code could be sent through the air using radio waves. At the beginning of the twentieth century Marconi established his own company to supply the equipment and trained operators needed on board ships, known as 'Marconi men'.

In February 1904 Marconi's company adopted the code 'CQD' as its standard code for ships in distress. CQ was already used by land-based telegraphs to indicate urgency, and 'D' was added by Marconi to mean distress. It was later popularly assumed to mean 'Come Quickly, Danger'. This code was widely used for many years, especially on British ships where Marconi had a virtual monopoly, but in 1906 an international conference agreed to adopt SOS instead. The Morse code for this signal is three dots, three dashes, three dots. So it is memorable, easier to send quickly and repeatedly, and instantly recognisable to those receiving it. This coding was pioneered in Germany and did not represent any particular phrase, but, like CQD,

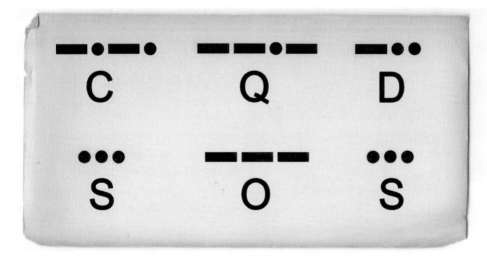

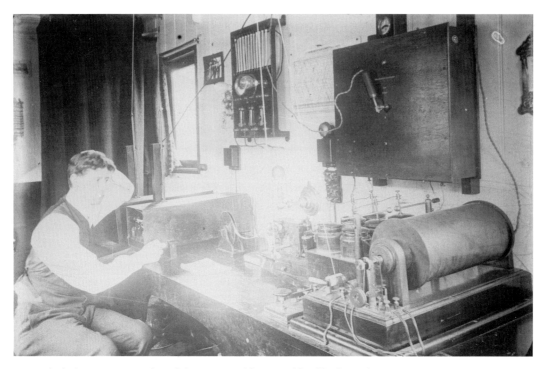

Marconi wireless operator on board the German ship *Deutschland* in the early 1900s.

Ship's wireless set with headphones and telegraph for sending Morse code.

it soon acquired its own backronym – 'Save Our Souls'.

It is impossible to calculate how many lives were saved at sea by the use of wireless telegraphy to call for assistance. Famously, the radio operators on RMS *Titanic* transmitted CQD when their ship first got into distress as it was still widely used, but later changed to SOS. This brought RMS *Carpathia* to their aid, saving all who survived. Contrary to popular belief, this was not the world's first maritime SOS. That honour belongs to 19-year-old wireless operator Stanley Coles of RMS *Slavonia*. His ship ran aground in the fog off the Azores on 10 June 1909. Two ships, SS *Prinzess Irene* and SS *Batavia*, answered Coles' call for assistance, enabling all the passengers and crew to be taken to mainland Europe. *Slavonia* itself was a complete write-off and had to be abandoned. Its captain was later severely reprimanded for sailing too fast in the foggy conditions and for being significantly off course.

Wireless telegraphy was largely succeeded by conventional radio ('radiotelephony') by the 1930s. This, of course, enabled human voices to be broadcast rather than Morse code.

60

Obelisk for submariners

A poignant tribute to the brave crews of early submarines

The early years of British submarines exposed their small crews to significant dangers. At the beginning of the twentieth century the idea of operating a military vessel underwater was still very new. The initial technology was primitive, and there was much to be learned about the design of these craft, their practical operation and their safety. It probably did not help that the Admiralty was initially suspicious of submarines and slow to recognise their potential. This meant that investment in their development was not as great as it might have been.

HMS *A1* was the first submarine designed and built in the UK. Launched in 1902, it unfortunately saw rather limited naval service. On 18 March 1904 the submarine was off the east coast of the Isle of Wight, under command of Lieutenant Loftus Manserch. It was taking part in military manoeuvres, including a practice 'stealth attack' on HMS *Juno*. Completely unaware of this, SS *Berwick Castle* steamed right through the area and hit something that at the time was believed to be a practice torpedo under the water. The captain reported it, and only then was it realised that the object must have been HMS *A1*, which had failed to resurface. The hole created in the sub by the collision meant that all eleven of the crew drowned. The submarine was salvaged and the bodies of the submariners retrieved for burial. The uniquely terrible way in which the crew died, trapped to drown in a metal tomb, attracted great public sympathy. HMS *A1*, however, was repaired and put back into service

as a training vessel, but was sunk a second time in 1911 while unmanned during an exercise. This time the wreck was not salvaged and it remains on the sea bed.

When the obelisk was first erected to honour the dead crew of HMS *A1*, the Royal Navy could not have foreseen that the remaining three sides

would soon be occupied with the names of more submariners with their own tragic tales of disaster.

On 16 February 1905 an explosion occurred aboard HMS *A5* at Queenstown (modern Cobh), Ireland. It was probably caused by petrol fumes being ignited by a spark, and it killed six of the crew of ten. In 1906 HMS *A8* suddenly dipped in the water while travelling on the surface with an open conning tower. The sea rushed in and the sub quickly foundered off Plymouth, drowning all fifteen crew. In 1912 HMS *A3* was running a dummy attack on HMS *Hazard* near the Isle of Wight when it accidentally collided with its target. Again the submarine sank, taking all fourteen hands to their deaths.

All four of these events are now commemorated on the obelisk, which stands at the Haslar Royal Naval Cemetery in Gosport.

Above: Large crowds gathered to pay their respects at the funeral of HMS *A1*'s crew.

Left: Ancient and modern – HMS *Victory* watches over an Edwardian submarine.

61

Photo of survivors

SS Hilda *was a winter shipwreck in which almost everyone on board froze to death*

Captain William Gregory was an experienced master mariner with around a thousand voyages across the English Channel to his name. He was a very cautious officer, attentive to danger. On 17 November 1905 he was in command of SS *Hilda*, taking passengers from Southampton to St Malo in France. He delayed his departure by nearly two hours because of fog and once at sea he anchored off the Isle of Wight at about 11pm to sit out further fog. The next morning there was heavy snow, causing yet more delay, but Captain Gregory was a patient man.

By 2pm on 19 November seaman James Grinter was told by a colleague that *Hilda* was off Jersey, and by 6pm they could see the lights of St Malo – but then it started to snow again and the shore lights vanished. The weather became squally and *Hilda* was constantly manoeuvred to stay clear of the land. Grinter went off duty at 8.30pm, by which time there was a heavy sea and the snow was continuing. Grinter went to sleep but at about 11pm he was awakened by the ship striking rocks. He rushed on deck, where Captain Gregory ordered the boats to be launched.

Unfortunately, three boats could not be deployed due to the proximity of the rocks, and a fourth was smashed to pieces by the elements

Saint-Malo
Naufrage du " HILDA " (19 novembre 1905)
Les six survivants

during launch. The passengers all donned lifejackets, and an attempt was being made to get off a portside boat when suddenly the stern of *Hilda* sank and everybody was washed off the deck into the freezing, tempestuous sea. It was so cold that those in the water stood no chance. Grinter and many others managed to reach the only mast still standing. 'The mate grasped the rigging and called me to climb up, and cook followed us,' he recollected; 'the starboard rigging was crowded with people.' Yet just after he had reached this refuge the ship broke in two with a mighty crash. At the same time *Hilda* heeled over dramatically, shaking off many of those on the rigging into the water. The ship rolled throughout the night, and one by one men died in the bitter cold.

The next morning SS *Ada* spotted the wreck and sent a boat to rescue the survivors, and a French pilot also sailed out to help. It was a difficult task in the strong wind and heavy sea. Between them they rescued James Grinter and five Breton passengers, who had travelled to the UK to sell onions. In the photograph Grinter is shown in the back row on the right.

The mate, a fireman and two passengers were found dead but still clinging to the rigging. Around 130 people died and the bodies of about seventy of them were found floating in the sea still in their lifejackets but killed by the extreme cold.

The broken wreck showing the mast that survivors clung to.

62

Postcard of half a ship

The wrecked stern of SS Suevic *was salvaged in 1907 and used to make a new ship*

The White Star Line had an almost inexorable tendency to lose prestigious ships. *Titanic*, lost in 1912, was of course the most infamous, but there were many others. In 1873 RMS *Atlantic* ran aground in a storm off Nova Scotia and lost all its lifeboats so that survivors had to swim ashore. A total of 535 people died – the worst loss of civilian life in a transatlantic shipwreck in the whole of the nineteenth century. In 1893 White Star's SS *Naronic* headed into the Atlantic and was never seen again; in 1909 the palatial RMS *Republic* sank after colliding with another ship. In 1916 *Britannic*, a sister vessel of *Titanic*, was serving as a wartime hospital ship when it struck a mine and sank.

Yet the story of SS *Suevic* is a remarkable one. On 17 March 1907 the ship was off southwest England, returning home from Melbourne in Australia. In strong night-time winds and rain that drastically cut visibility, the officers were unable to ascertain their position and relied on sighting the Lizard lighthouse, Cornwall, to

steer a safe course. When the lighthouse was eventually spotted, the *Suevic* was 16 miles ahead of its estimated position and, despite a last-minute attempt to alter course, the ship steamed powerfully onto the rocks at almost full speed.

Fortunately, the ship was trapped on the rocks in relatively shallow water and was in no immediate danger of sinking. Captain Thomas Jones ordered that distress rockets be fired and RNLI lifeboats from four different stations raced to the rescue. It was to be the greatest saving of life in the RNLI's history, with 456 passengers and crew rescued over an exhausting sixteen hours; the small lifeboats were powered only by rowers. Incredibly, no lives were lost and six men were awarded RNLI medals for their bravery.

Yet the extraordinary tale does not end there. Attempts to salvage the entire ship failed, but White Star calculated that if the stern alone could

be saved, it would be financially worthwhile. Accordingly, carefully placed dynamite charges were used to separate the bows, still trapped on the rocks, from the stern, which was successfully refloated and taken to Southampton. Meanwhile in Belfast, shipbuilders Harland & Wolff built a new set of bows which were towed to Southampton, where the two halves were joined.

The public was fascinated by this story, which demonstrated the ingenuity of British shipbuilders, and many postcards were produced such as the ones shown here to illustrate what had happened.

Suevic re-entered service in January 1908, less than a year after the disaster, and sailed for another thirty-four years. In the Second World War, under a new name, it was deliberately scuttled to prevent it falling into the hands of the Germans.

The *Suevic* ashore in the gloom.

A new set of bows (left) being joined to the salvaged stern (right) at Southampton.

63

Former White Star Line offices, Southampton

Here people queued to discover if their relatives had survived the sinking of RMS Titanic

In 1912 this small building was suddenly the focus of attention. Radio messages shared between ships in the Atlantic broke the news to the city of Southampton on 15 April that *Titanic* had foundered. It later emerged that around 1,500 people had died. But who had survived and who had died? *Titanic* had an estimated crew of 908 people, and of these 724 came from Southampton. With nowhere else to turn, desperate local families gathered outside the White Star office to await news of their loved ones. Yet they had to wait an agonising five days before a definitive list of survivors could be produced. Those who survived had had to be picked up, transported to safety, identified, logged and reported back to the UK. This took time.

When they had all the information available, White Star staff wrote out a list of all the known survivors on large sheets of paper, affixed these to the railings outside their office, then retreated. Local people crowded around to discover relief

or sorrow, but it was mainly sorrow. It was worse than anyone feared: of the 696 crewmembers who died, 549 came from Southampton. The city was plunged into despair.

Given the scale of this tragedy, Southampton is understandably noted for its many *Titanic* memorials. Probably the most famous is the bronze and stone depiction of the engineering officers 'who showed their high conception of duty and their heroism by remaining at their posts'. There is a touching memorial to *Titanic's* musicians, who continued playing as the ship went down. It's a replica because the original was destroyed by air raids in 1940, but it shows the ship sinking, with notes of a hymn and the names of the players. In the civic centre is a memorial to the ship's postal workers: it was fashioned from *Titanic's*

Memorial to *Titanic's* engineer officers.

spare propeller, which shipbuilders Harland & Wolff donated. Holyrood Church houses a public fountain erected to commemorate all the crewmembers who died; it is surmounted by *Titanic* itself slicing through the waves.

However, four Southampton crewmen fortuitously escaped the icy clutches of the Atlantic. The brothers Alfred, Bertram and Thomas Slade were in a pub with their friend, Alfred Penney. They had all signed on as *Titanic*

crew, but they left it to the last minute to board the ship because it was just around the corner. With just a few minutes before departure they knew they could make it, but then a train blocked their path for what seemed like an age. By the time they reached the waterside, the gangplank was being withdrawn. All four of them pleaded and protested, but they were too late. Their whole lives had been changed immeasurably by a slow-moving train.

64

Press photo of Arthur Rostron and Molly Brown

Honouring the man who led the rescue of Titanic's survivors

Arthur Rostron was captain of *Carpathia* – the vessel that was first on the scene to take on board survivors from *Titanic*'s lifeboats. At top speed, he defiantly ploughed through seas where ice was known to be drifting. He knew he was taking a risk with his own ship by doing this, but it enabled him to save more than seven hundred people. In the United States Rostron was presented with many awards, including a Congressional Gold Medal and the American Cross of Honor. The press photo below shows him receiving a silver trophy from *Titanic* survivor Margaret 'Molly' Brown on behalf of the passengers that he rescued.

It was common after a rescue at sea for employers, national institutions or grateful owners of ships to give financial awards or gifts to the rescuers as a token of their gratitude. On top of this, the people who survived a wreck frequently rewarded those who had saved them

from a watery grave, if they had the means to do so, and quite often there would be a public collection for particularly courageous acts.

In Victorian times the government's Board of Trade made awards for meritorious or heroic conduct. For example, Charles Newman, captain of *Albion* from Cardiff rescued the crew of *Potentate* in 1863 as the ship was sinking beneath their feet. He was awarded a telescope valued at £5 15s 6d. Foreign governments might do the same. Captain John Piton from Jersey was awarded a gold chronometer by US president Abraham Lincoln after saving the shipwrecked crew of the American vessel *Richard Mosse* in 1862.

There were medals available from various UK charities to honour bravery at sea, such as those from the RNLI and Royal Humane Society (chapters 25 and 50), as well as from the insurer Lloyd's of London. The main state awards that could be granted for bravery at sea were the Board of Trade Medal for

Captain John Piton was honoured by Abraham Lincoln.

Saving Life at Sea (more usually known as the 'Sea Gallantry Medal'), the Albert Medal (now called the George Cross) and the British Empire Medal.

Strangely, despite rescuing so many *Titanic* victims, Captain Rostron did not receive a UK state award for his efforts, although the Liverpool Shipwreck and Humane Society presented him with a gold medal, and eight of his crew received silver medals. However, he was knighted in 1926 after a distinguished career that saw him command ships in the First World War and become the longstanding captain of the celebrated Cunard liner RMS *Mauretania*.

Rostron was a Lancastrian but when he died he was – fittingly enough – buried near Southampton, *Titanic*'s spiritual home, where a road was later named after him.

65

A ship ablaze

Caught on camera by a rescue vessel, the burning SS Volturno *threatened the lives of over 650 people*

The *Titanic* tragedy had created a demand for ships to carry sufficient lifeboat places for everyone on board. This requirement was not agreed internationally until 1914, but some ship-owners were early adopters. SS *Volturno* had enough boats and rafts to take 1,093 people, and it carried 1,511 life-jackets and 23 lifebuoys. This was more than adequate for the 561 passengers and 93 crew on board when the ship left Rotterdam on 2 October 1913. However, other important aspects of maritime safety were still being ignored, as the frightening events on *Volturno* illustrate.

Early on the morning of 9 October a fire started in *Volturno*'s cargo hold and the alarm was raised. There were two explosions which disabled the steering, and the flames killed at least four crewmen. Fire-fighting began, and boats were lowered despite the heavy sea. Four were launched carrying people: two turned over during launch, one was crushed under the rocking *Volturno*, and a fourth got away with up to fifty people on board but was never seen again. Other empty boats were smashed during launch.

Alarmingly, almost all the 134 people who died were killed in the lifeboats. Nearly everyone

who stayed on the burning ship survived and were rescued by one of the twelve steamships that soon answered *Volturno*'s distress calls and came to its aid.

The cause of the blaze was never officially established. However, *Volturno* was carrying 144 barrels of barium superoxide powder. At the subsequent inquiry, an expert rubbed the chemical lightly between pieces of wood and it spontaneously burst into flames. *Volturno* had faced some rough seas that would have agitated the cargo, and the court discovered that at least two other ships carrying this hazardous substance had gone up in smoke in recent years.

The court also noted the inadequate nature of *Volturno*'s crew training for launching boats in an emergency, known as 'boat drill'. This almost universal problem was related to the fact that most crewmembers were only employed for one voyage at a time because ship-owners did not want to pay for them when they weren't at sea. This meant there was no opportunity to train crews in-between voyages, and at the commencement of a voyage there was too much going on to do training. Once the ship was at sea the time available depended on what else the crew were required to do. Every ship had different types and locations for lifeboats, and yet boat drill was often cursory and incomplete. Hence crews were ill-prepared to launch lifeboats properly in practice or to manage them once afloat.

The problem of non-permanent contracts for crewmembers did not change until the Second World War, whilst modern international regulations for the safe carrying of dangerous goods were not agreed until the 1960s.

66

Newspaper front page announcing the death of Laurence Irving

A famous actor and his wife lost on Empress of Ireland *in 1914*

Laurence Irving was the son of Victorian theatre giant Sir Henry Irving, and he and his wife Mabel both had successful acting careers of their own. He was also a playwright, and in May 1914 the couple had just concluded a highly successful tour of Canada, starring principally in Laurence's own play *The Typhoon*. They embarked on RMS *Empress of Ireland* on 28 May, the ship departing Quebec in the late afternoon and sailing down the St Lawrence river towards the Atlantic.

The river became foggy after midnight. *Empress of Ireland* and a Norwegian collier, SS *Storstad*, were aware of each other and were initially a few miles apart, but as the fog thickened they lost visual contact. They kept up fog whistles and displayed lights, but somehow, with alarming rapidity, *Storstad* loomed out of the murk and rammed *Empress* amidships. *Storstad* acted like a giant tin opener, ripping a huge gash in the side of the other ship.

Empress filled with water so quickly there was no time to close its watertight doors. People on the lower decks drowned, and those who reached the main deck tried to get into lifeboats. Some of the starboard boats were launched, but the ship was listing rapidly and none of the port lifeboats could be deployed. The lights failed soon afterwards, and then the ship turned over onto its starboard side, allowing hundreds to climb out onto it. Many sat down together here, but any hopes that

the ship had stabilised in this position were soon dashed and it suddenly slipped below the water. It was less than fifteen minutes since the collision.

There had been approximately 1,477 people on board *Empress*, and around 1,015 died. *Storstad*

LOST IN THE "EMPRESS OF IRELAND": MR. LAURENCE IRVING, THE ACTOR, AND HIS WIFE, MISS MABEL HACKNEY.

remained afloat and lost no one. The crew of each ship blamed the other, but at the official inquiry *Storstad* was found at fault. However, the captain of *Empress* probably altered course in a way that *Storstad* could not have fully seen in the fog, nor predicted.

Newspaper accounts of the disaster relate how the Irvings were asleep in their cabin when the collision happened. Laurence reached the main deck, but somehow they had become separated. He knew Mabel could not

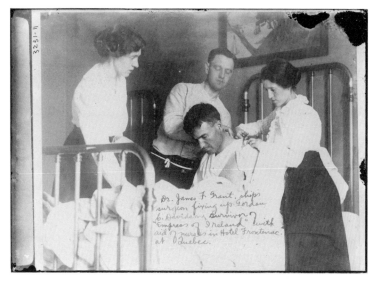

Injured survivor Gordon Davidson being treated by a surgeon and nurses at Quebec

swim and ran back to find her. He was able to get his wife on deck, still clad in her nightclothes, and they put on their lifebelts, poor Mabel crying. They reached the side of the ship after it had rolled over and, just before the ship went down, husband and wife were seen to kiss and hug each other.

When Laurence's body was washed ashore he was still clutching a piece of his wife's nightdress.

Empress of Ireland.

67

German publicity image of U-boat U-9 crew

The submarine that unnerved the Royal Navy in 1914

Shortly after the commencement of the First World War, Germany was able to celebrate an important sea victory. The text on this postcard issued at the time reads: 'Our heroes! The happy returning crew of U-boat *U-9* with their commander Kapitänleutnant Weddigen, after their achievement on 22nd Sept 1914 of sinking three English cruisers.'

On that date Otto Weddigen and his U-boat crew were off the Dutch coast at first light when they spotted three Royal Navy ships, part of the Seventh Cruiser Squadron guarding the eastern entrance to the English Channel. Weddigen successfully targeted HMS *Aboukir* with a torpedo and managed to do so without being seen. The British assumed that their ship had struck a mine and the other two cruisers closed with *Aboukir* as it sank to lend assistance. This allowed Weddigen to fire two torpedoes at HMS *Hogue*, which was so badly damaged that it went down very quickly. But this time the U-boat had been seen. HMS *Cressy* gave chase and attempted to ram the U-boat, but missed. When the cruiser turned back to rescue sailors in the water, Weddigen fired three torpedoes at the retreating foe and

Unsere Helden !
Die glücklich zurückgekehrte Mannschaft des Unterseebootes „U 9" mit ihrem Kommandanten Kapitänleutnant Weddigen, durch deren Heldentat am 22. Sept. 1914, 3 engl. Kreuzer in Grund gebohrt wurden.

Cressy speedily capsized, floating upside down for some time before going to the bottom. It was one-sided carnage. The British had been completely out-thought. Over 1,400 men lost their lives.

Fifteen-year-old Royal Navy midshipman Kit Wykeham Musgrave miraculously survived all three sinkings. He was originally on *Aboukir* and dived overboard as it went down; he had just clambered aboard *Hogue* when it too was torpedoed. Having swum to apparent safety on HMS *Cressy*, he couldn't believe it when this ship also sank beneath him. In the water for the third time, he was soon exhausted but found a large piece of floating wood to cling to and was later picked up by a Dutch trawler.

The British were not well-prepared for dealing with enemy submarines, known as U-boats from the German '*unterseeboot*' (under-sea boat). Yet they became the major method by which Germany waged war at sea. The Admiralty knew it had to change tactics, and fast.

At home in Germany, Weddigen was awarded the Iron Cross and became the first of a number of celebrated U-boat commanders, fêted wherever he went. Within a month he had claimed another victim, HMS *Hawke*, and in the following year he sank four merchant ships and damaged two more. However, his luck soon ran out. In March 1915, when in command of *U-29*, he surfaced in the path of HMS *Dreadnought*, which chased and rammed the U-boat, slicing it in two. There were no survivors.

Weddigen was a trailblazer. More successful submarine commanders were to follow, most notably Lothar von Arnauld de la Perière, who was to sink a staggering 195 British and Allied ships.

Otto Weddigen and his wife.

68

Ship's propeller

One of four that were fitted to RMS Lusitania: *its loss to a U-boat incensed the world*

Weighing 22.5 tons, this propeller went to the bottom of the Atlantic in 1915 along with the rest of *Lusitania*, and lay there for sixty-seven years until salvaged. It is now on display outside Merseyside Maritime Museum in Liverpool, the ship's home port. There is still a service of commemoration there every year on 7 May, the anniversary of the ship's sinking.

When launched in 1906, *Lusitania* was the largest vessel afloat and it was a very fast ship: it broke the Blue Riband record for the fastest crossing of the Atlantic on only its second voyage to the United States. In all, *Lusitania* would make more than two hundred transatlantic crossings before its sad demise.

Returning from New York in 1915, *Lusitania* was approaching the coast of Ireland when some passengers on deck saw a German submarine's conning tower a few hundred yards to starboard. A few even claimed to see the torpedo that U-boat *UB-20* fired, as it raced toward them. It struck *Lusitania* just below the bridge. All over the ship people raced to get up on deck. In the second class dining room, Mrs Phoebe Amory recalled pushing through the tightly packed, fearful crowd that blocked the stairway to the upper decks:

Someone shouted 'We have been torpedoed', and I realized for the first time that we were doomed. As I fought my way up the stairs, I was thrown on my knees three times. Near the top of the stairway there was an officer shouting 'keep cool', and his words seemed to have the desired effect.

It seemed to take hours to reach the deck and fresh air, but in reality it was just a few minutes. Once there, the unnatural slope of the deck revealed their perilous situation, and Mrs Amory feared she would slide overboard. The list hampered the launching of lifeboats because they either swung away from the deck, out of reach, or swung in-board so that it was difficult to lower them into the water.

The screams of the women and children were terrible to hear. Wives were being torn from their husbands and lifted into the lifeboats. Children, who in the terrible crush of humans, had become separated from their parents, were being handed from man to man and on into the boats. Women were fainting and falling to the deck, only to be carried overboard by their own weight.

Mrs Amory had just about given up looking for a lifebelt when a young man bravely gave her his own. He helped her into it and adjusted it for her. Few of *Lusitania*'s lifeboats were launched successfully. Most couldn't be launched; of those that were, some tipped their passengers into the sea on lowering because of the *Lusitania*'s list, and, distressingly, some were filled with passengers but still secured to the liner as it went down.

Mrs Amory ended up floating alone in the sea, grateful for the lifebelt that saved her, and

Lusitania at sea.

was eventually rescued by an overloaded lifeboat. Bodies floated past them – men, women and children – 'it was terrible to look upon children, oh, such little children, floating away out there on the ocean'. The sinking was responsible for the deaths of around 1,200 passengers and crew. Yet astonishingly, despite the ship going down in just eighteen minutes, 764 people were rescued and survived. The young man who saved Mrs Amory by giving her his lifebelt was not among the survivors.

69

The 'Lusitania medal'

German propaganda disaster after sinking luxury liner

In the aftermath of the sinking of *Lusitania*, a different war-within-a-war took place: a war of propaganda. Germany argued that *Lusitania* was a legitimate target, alleging that it carried munitions, and that the ship-owners, Cunard, and the British government knew the vessel would enter a war zone. Germany had, in fact, even put warnings in American newspapers urging passengers not to board. However, the rest of the world were appalled by the sinking, even neutral nations.

Germany's international reputation was not helped by the actions of one of its own citizens, Karl Goetz. He produced a *Lusitania* medal for private sale. The obverse shows the ship sinking, crammed with illegal guns for the war effort, and bearing the admonitory legend '*Keine Bann Ware!*' ('No contraband!'). Beneath this is the text '*Der Grossdampfer Lusitania Durch Ein Deutches*

Tauchboot Versenkt 5 May 1915' ('The great steamship *Lusitania* has been sunk by German submarines 5 May 1915').

The reverse shows a personification of Death as a skeleton, selling tickets to passengers from a Cunard booth. One of the passengers holds a newspaper warning about U-boats. Above this scene is the text '*Geschaft Uber Alles*' ('Business above all').

Goetz intended to disparage the British for supposedly using *Lusitania* to carry munitions, and Cunard for making money from the public when Germany had warned that all British ships were a target. However, a Goetz medal found its way to Britain, where copies were made and sold as examples of Germany glorifying an atrocity. Boxes holding the replicas carried this text: 'This indicates the true feeling that the War Lords endeavour to stimulate, and is proof positive that

such crimes are not merely regarded favourably, but are given every encouragement.' Anger was further fuelled by the fact that Goetz put the wrong date for the sinking on his medal – 5 May instead of 7 May – which made it look as if Germany had premeditated the *Lusitania* attack. German warnings about the dangers of their own U-boats were dismissed as seeking 'to propound the theory that if a murderer warns his victims of his intention, the guilt of the crime will rest with the victim, not the murderer'.

Germany decisively lost the propaganda war over *Lusitania* worldwide, but most particularly in the United States on account of the many American citizens who died in the sinking.

The attack on *Lusitania* is still the subject of controversy even today. Some people argue that the vessel became a target by carrying weaponry, or that Britain deliberately set the ship up as a target to provoke the United States into entering the war. It is probably true that *Lusitania* was one of a number of outrages that eventually caused America to join hostilities, but that was two years after the loss of *Lusitania*.

Some passengers on *Lusitania* said that they saw the U-boat just before the attack.

70

A badge for a lost son

William Abbott's ship went down with all hands at the Battle of Jutland in 1916

George and Martha Abbott welcomed their son William into the world with joy in 1886, but sadly Martha died suddenly only four years later. As a young lad William helped his father, George, braiding twine at their home in Dorset, yet it wasn't the kind of employment he wanted. He worked on a nearby pig farm for a few months as a swine-shed boy, but when he was 16 he decided to leave home and enlist in the Royal Navy.

When the First World War broke out in 1914, William had more than eight years' experience as a seaman, and in April of that year he joined the armoured cruiser HMS *Black Prince*, which

in 1916 was attached to the Royal Navy's prestigious Grand Fleet.

It had been expected that sooner or later the Grand Fleet would meet the German High Seas Fleet, and the British would then destroy the enemy as Nelson had done at Trafalgar a century earlier. However, this was not what happened when the two fleets engaged at the Battle of Jutland. It was an engagement in three stages over two days, starting on 31 May, but there was no decisive winner. Both fleets retired from the action and both sides claimed victory.

At the conclusion of Jutland, the tactical advantage lay with the British – they had forced

the German fleet back to their home ports and could maintain their blockade on supplies which was to play a vital role in Britain winning the war. Nevertheless, it didn't feel like a victory: Britain lost fourteen ships to Germany's eleven, and more than twice as many men (6,784 compared to Germany's 3,039).

One of the men who died was George's son, William. HMS *Black Prince* was sent ahead of the main fleet as part of the First Cruiser Squadron, but lost contact with the squadron. That night *Black Prince* continued to seek its British counterparts, but in the darkness it inadvertently blundered into the middle of the German fleet. The captain realised his error and put the ship about, but it was too late. The ill-fated British vessel was lit up by enemy searchlights and multiple ships opened fire at close quarters. The end came quickly: *Black Prince* was seriously damaged and sank, catching fire or even exploding before the end. All 857 men on board were killed: there were no survivors.

Since the opening days of the war, William's father – like all parents of young men fighting for their country – had dreaded the arrival of the post each day. One morning in June he reluctantly opened a small envelope from the Admiralty thrust through his letterbox, and read: 'It is my painful duty to inform you ... It is deeply regretted . . . he must, in the absence of evidence to the contrary, be regarded as having lost his life.'

George endured the matchless grief of a parent whose child dies before they do. His son lay somewhere at the bottom of the North Sea, so there was no body to bring home – no last goodbye, no funeral, no grave.

In the absence of a gravestone, George created his own personal memorial for his son. A patriotic badge with red, white and blue enamelling was sold as a blank by the John Bull company so that it could be engraved in memory of a loved one. William's father chose these words: 'In memory of a dear and only son, William Abbott, HMS Black Prince 31/5/16.' He was just 29 years old.

Britain's Bulwarks in Action, May 31st, 1916
Sinking of German Battle Cruiser

Contemporary postcard extolling the sinking of a German ship at Jutland, but the battle was not the unequivocal British success that had been expected.

71

In memoriam *card for Lord Kitchener*

The most famous victim of a wartime shipwreck

Only five days after the Royal Navy's failure to win a decisive victory at Jutland came more distressing news. Lord Kitchener, Secretary of State for War, was dead – drowned in the wreckage of HMS *Hampshire* on 5 June 1916. Over seven hundred others died with him, and only twelve of the crew survived.

Kitchener was a controversial figure amongst the political and military hierarchy. The king may have called him an 'old and valued friend', but some thought him irascible, controlling and difficult. However, to the nation as a whole he was the personification of British defiance. The most iconic image of the entire conflict shows Kitchener's pointing finger and steely gaze while demanding that he wants *you* for the war effort. He was widely lauded as the Empire's Greatest Soldier, so the loss of Kitchener at sea plunged Britain into shock. It was a significant blow to morale that some later said was their lowest ebb.

The Secretary of State had been heading a delegation to Russia to reassure the Tsar about Britain's support, and to discuss military tactics and the provision of arms. After Kitchener's ship left Scapa Flow, a last-minute change of route in a Force 9 gale took the warship around Orkney into waters that had not been checked for mines. HMS *Hampshire* struck a mine laid by U-boat *U-75* only the week before on its first-ever mission. The ship immediately started to sink by the bows, and the storm made launching

lifeboats impossible: they smashed against the sides or overturned. Within fifteen minutes the mighty *Hampshire* had disappeared beneath the waves, taking Kitchener with it.

After the ship went down, there were initially hundreds of men in the water. Many used lifebelts, but three rafts had been launched that each had between fifty and ninety men on board. However, it was bitterly cold and the survivors reported that men gradually died from exhaustion, exposure and the cold.

Leading Seaman Charles Rogerson was a survivor, and afterwards gave interviews:

I got away on one of the rafts, and we had a terrible five hours in the water. It was so rough that the sea beat down on us, and many men were killed by the buffeting they received. Many others died from the fearful cold. I was quite benumbed. An almost overwhelming desire to sleep came upon us, and to get over this we thumped each other on the back, for no man who went to sleep ever woke again. When men died it was just as though they were going to sleep. One man stood upright

Charles Rogerson (left) and William Cashman (right), two of HMS *Hampshire*'s survivors.

on a raft for five hours with dead lying all around him. Another man died in my arms. As we got near the shore the situation got worse. The wind was blowing towards the shore, and the fury of the sea dashed our raft against the rocks with tremendous force. Many were killed in this way, and one raft was overturned three times. I do not know quite how I got ashore. All the feeling had gone out of me.

Even reaching the shore was no guarantee of survival: many bodies were found with their fingernails ripped away by desperate attempts to grab hold of rocks in the rough seas. This was an agonising detail for the grieving relatives.

Rogerson was the last survivor to see the Secretary of State: 'Lord Kitchener went down with the ship,' he said. 'He did not leave her.' In the heroic tradition that would be expected of such a man, Kitchener was reported as standing on the quarterdeck talking calmly to officers while the ship was sinking. His body was never found.

Lord Kitchener's famous encouragement to enlist.

72

Souvenir of a captured enemy vessel

Postcard of mine-laying U-boat UC-5 – mines were an important cause of ship losses

The torpedoes and deck guns of U-boats sank by far the most British ships in the First World War, but German sea mines were the next most common cause of casualties – accounting for around 260 vessels. Lord Kitchener was the most famous victim of a U-boat mine, but they were indiscriminate: sinking fishing trawlers and hospital ships, as well as military vessels and merchant ships carrying war supplies.

At the beginning of the war many sea lanes were mined by the British and the Germans. For example, the approaches to German ports were protected in this way. The locations of these 'set pieces' were often known by both sides,

even if the precise layout was not, and a single mine could wreck even a large ship. During the Dardanelles campaign in 1915 the battleship HMS *Irresistible* was sunk by a sea mine, and although many of the crew were saved, about 150 men lost their lives.

However, when U-boats started to lay sea mines, it was the unpredictability of their location that caught out many British ships. A U-boat might lay a string of new mines overnight in a location where there had been none the day before.

The British captured mine-laying U-boat *UC-5* in 1916. It was a significant coup, because *UC-5* had been very successful in

The crew of SS *Swiftsure*; this cargo ship was wrecked by a mine laid by *UC-40* off Orkney in September 1917.

wrecking Allied shipping. In particular, one of *UC-5*'s mines had caused the hospital ship HMHS *Anglia* to founder in 1915, taking 129 wounded soldiers and crewmen to their deaths. The circumstances of *UC-5*'s capture also demonstrated that U-boats were not infallible. The commander of *UC-5*, Ulrich Mohrbutter, set out to lay mines near the Shipwash light vessel off the coast of Harwich. Instead, to his mortification, Mohrbutter ran aground. He was forced to abandon ship and set charges to blow up the submarine, but they did not detonate.

UC-5 was salvaged and exhibited on the Thames, where thousands of people paid a small

fee to look around. It was good propaganda. The exhibition and mementoes such as this postcard demonstrated to the public that Britain understood the German technology and could best it, even if a significant element of good fortune was required. Additionally, it suggested the devious nature of the enemy: laying underwater bombs to destroy unsuspecting British ships in a manner that could be portrayed as underhand or 'unfair'.

This longitudinal section of *UC-5* shows how mines were stored in conduits from which they could be released when required from the underside of the U-boat.

73

Aerial photo of a sinking hospital ship

Hospital ships such as Gloucester Castle *were considered*
fair game by some U–boat commanders

This rather grainy but dramatic wartime photo was issued to the press by the Ministry of Information and reproduced with the caption: 'War on hospital ships: were evidence wanting of German attacks on British Red Cross ships, here the camera supplies it.'

In March 1917 *Gloucester Castle* was torpedoed by U-boat *UB-32* off the Isle of Wight. Fortunately, in this case the crew and the wounded were rescued with the loss of only three lives. The ship did not sink completely and was salvaged a fortnight later and towed back to port to be repaired.

However, during the First World War a total of eight British hospital ships were deliberately targeted by U-boat torpedoes, and a further five sank due to mines laid by U-boats. Britain sank just one German hospital ship during the war, SS *Tabora*, which was almost certainly masquerading as a hospital ship but was really a transport vessel for military supplies. The Royal Navy surgeon who was given permission to inspect this ship found only one patient on board, and he was still wearing his trousers underneath the bedsheets!

British hospital ships were designated HMHS – His Majesty's Hospital Ship – and

Above: Gold nuggets have been found on the shore where *Royal Charter* sank (chapter 38)

Right: Guze Ruggier who courageously swam ashore from *Royal Charter* with a rope

THE UNFORTUNATE LONDON.

A mug produced to commemorate the shocking loss of SS *London* in 1866 (chapter 40)

Window in Liverpool Cathedral honouring Mary Ann Rogers, who bravely surrendered her life when SS *Stella* was wrecked in 1899 (chapter 58)

Propeller in Liverpool salvaged from the wreck of RMS *Lusitania* (chapter 68)

Badge made to honour William Abbott's sacrifice at the Battle of Jutland (chapter 70)

Right: Passenger
badge from TSS
Athenia, sunk by
u-boat in 1939
(chapter 81)

Below: Book of
remembrance for HMS
Hood victims in Boldre
Church (chapter 84)

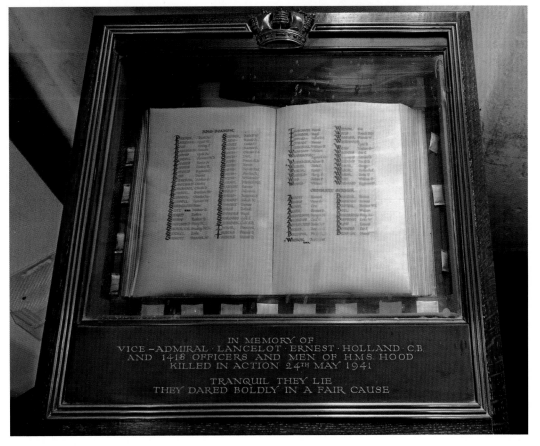

IN MEMORY OF
VICE-ADMIRAL LANCELOT ERNEST HOLLAND C.B.
AND 1418 OFFICERS AND MEN OF H.M.S. HOOD
KILLED IN ACTION 24TH MAY 1941

TRANQUIL THEY LIE
THEY DARED BOLDLY IN A FAIR CAUSE

HMS *Belfast*, moored on the Thames (chapter 88)

The Tower Hill Memorial to merchant seamen lost in the Great War (chapter 93)

A dead guillemot; seabirds are vulnerable to fuel emanating from wrecks (chapter 94)

The RNLI memorial to those who gave their lives attempting to rescue others (chapter 99)

The iconic Titanic Belfast museum (chapter 100)

IN PROUD AND GRATEFUL MEMORY
OF THOSE WHO GAVE THEIR LIVES
IN THE HOSPITAL SHIP
GLENART CASTLE.
PLEASE REMEMBER,
MASTER LT. CMDR. BURT, MATRON KATY BEAUFOY,
THE SHIPS OFFICERS, CREW AND MEDICAL STAFF
WHO DIED WHEN THEIR SHIP WAS TORPEDOED
BY UC56 IN THE EARLY HOURS OF 26th FEB. 1918.
THE SHIP LIES 20 MILES WNW FROM THIS STONE.
FOR THOSE IN PERIL ON THE SEA
R.I.P.
DEDICATED 26.02.2002

A memorial to the *Glenart Castle* victims was unveiled at Hartland Point in 2002.

according to international convention were unarmed, painted white with red crosses on their hulls, and were brightly illuminated at night. They were forbidden to carry military supplies or troops on active duty, and were allowed to be inspected by the enemy. The deliberate targeting of hospital ships by Germany contravened international law and provoked outrage in Britain. Although not all U-boat commanders complied, they were urged to consider any British ship a fair target during the period of unrestricted U-boat warfare.

The most notorious example was the sinking of HMHS *Glenart Castle* in 1918. It was clearly marked as a hospital ship, and brightly illuminated at night, yet Wilhelm Kiesewetter in command of U-boat *UC-56* targeted the vessel and sank it with a torpedo in the Bristol

Channel. Most of the people on board were sleeping at the time of the attack. Furthermore, the blast destroyed many of the lifeboats, the sea was rough and the vessel sank quickly so there was great loss of life. The death toll in the sinking amounted to around 160 people, including the captain, eight nurses, forty-seven medical orderlies and ninety-nine patients. Amongst the losses was also the ship's matron, Katy Beaufoy.

At least one victim was found floating on the surface with gunshot wounds, suggesting that Kiesewetter had attempted to kill survivors after the initial attack to cover up the massacre. Britain tried to pursue him for war crimes in 1918, but, having detained him, they were forced to release him due to the terms of the armistice.

74

Image of officers and cadets before a final voyage

The crew of Dee *were destined to lose their ship to the German* Wolf

This photograph shows 64-year-old Jack Rugg, captain of *Dee*, standing in the centre of the back row, wearing a flat cap. The other men are his officers: the first mate, Jean Marton, is third from the left in the middle row, and seated on the deck are two apprentice officers or cadets.

Sailing ships, such as the three-masted barque *Dee*, still had a mercantile role during the 1910s because they were cheaper to operate than steamships. They had smaller crews and did not require fuel, so could transport non-perishable goods over long distances at an economic rate, even though their cargo capacity was limited. For example, they often carried wool from Australia to Britain. This trading role meant that sailing ships were still considered legitimate targets by the Germans

in the First World War, as Captain Rugg was to discover.

Although U-boats sank the majority of British ships in the First World War, they were not the only threat. In particular, a small number of German armed cruisers operated very successfully to capture or destroy merchant vessels. These unmarked lone attackers were known as raiders. They were often disguised as merchant ships and only revealed their true identity at the last moment when it was too late for their prey to flee.

SMS *Wolf* was a raider that sneaked out of the German port of Kiel in 1916, evading the Royal Navy patrols. Under its commanding officer, Karl August Nerger, *Wolf* set about destroying British and Allied merchant ships in a single cruise around Africa, India and Australia that lasted a remarkable 451 days.

On 30 March 1917 Nerger sighted *Dee* about 400 miles off Cape Leeuwin, Australia, and surfaced ahead of the ship. He ordered the vessel to halt. Captain Rugg had no choice but to stop. *Wolf* was much more powerful than his veteran

sailing ship, which had been built in 1885. Nerger could have done what so many U-boat commanders did and simply destroy the unarmed ship with its crew on board. However, his policy was to capture ships, loot them for cargo and fuel, and take the crew prisoner. The nineteen seamen and officers of *Dee* were marched aboard *Wolf*, and shortly afterwards Captain Rugg watched with horror as his beloved ship became target practice for *Wolf*'s gun crew. He wept as the wrecked vessel sank before his eyes.

There followed a long, cramped and dangerous journey home. Prisoners and German crew alike were never sure if their unmarked ship would be targeted by U-boats or the British. Eventually, in 1918, *Wolf* made it back to Germany, where a victorious Nerger was given Germany's highest decoration by the Kaiser personally. Nerger handed over 467 Merchant Navy prisoners from the thirty-seven ships he had attacked. The crewmen from *Dee* were dispersed across five different prisoner of war camps. However, despite being 65 years of age, Captain Rugg survived the war and returned to the UK.

Karl Nerger, the commander of *Wolf*.

75

Reconnaissance photo of three ships wrecked at Zeebrugge

British ships wrecked deliberately to thwart enemy U-boats in 1918

Not all ship losses are unintentional. Vessels have been wrecked to form the basis of a breakwater, for example, or to act as an artificial reef. In wartime a ship may be scuttled to prevent it falling into the hands of the enemy. This was the fate of HMS *Sapphire* in 1696: trapped in a Newfoundland harbour, Captain Cleasby sank his ship rather than let the French have it.

But in 1918 the British had a very different purpose in mind when they planned to wreck ships at the Belgian port of Zeebrugge. This port allowed access to the U-boat base at Bruges, which was further inland, and a raid was conceived in which three ageing naval vessels – HMS *Intrepid*, *Iphigenia* and *Thetis* – would be sunk in the narrow channel used by German submarines in an attempt to prevent their access.

These cruisers were filled with concrete so that they would sink quickly and would be difficult to move once on the sea bed.

The men on board were all volunteers, having agreed to participate in an initially unspecified 'special service'. The raid on Zeebrugge was planned, and even begun, on more than one occasion before its eventual completion on 23 April 1918. The success of the plan depended on many factors operating in its favour, not least the weather.

The three old cruisers were never intended to operate in isolation, as they would have been sitting ducks. A raid was organised on the nearby mole or causeway at Zeebrugge, headed by HMS *Vindictive*, and another at the adjacent port of Ostend to block the U-boat channel in use there. The attack on the mole failed because a change in wind direction blew away the smokescreen designed to hide *Vindictive*, and the sailors and marines landing to disable German guns suffered heavy casualties and could not achieve their full mission. As a result, the Germans could concentrate almost their full firepower on *Intrepid*, *Iphigenia* and *Thetis* as they approached.

It is a great credit to all involved that the three cruisers were scuttled relatively near their intended positions, despite coming under such intense fire. However, *Thetis* hit an obstruction and did not even make it to the canal entrance. The two remaining ships were sunk close to their anticipated locations within the channel, but were not quite in the right place. The raid on nearby Ostend was a complete failure, with neither blocking ship even reaching its destination.

Although the Zeebrugge raid was portrayed as a plucky British victory at the time, it was not in fact a success. Within days, the Germans had dredged a new deep channel around the wrecks of *Intrepid* and *Iphigenia* which allowed U-boats to continue using the port. Nonetheless it was the scene of some outstanding bravery, with no fewer than eight Victoria Crosses being awarded.

Four survivors of the Zeebrugge raid smiling for the camera despite their injuries.

76

Merchant Navy torpedo cuff badge

Badge of honour for shipwreck survivors

Many Merchant Navy employees lost their lives to the U-boats in the First World War but, fortunately, there were also plenty who managed to escape before their ships went down. In 1918 the government introduced a method of honouring crewmembers who had survived the sinking of a commercial ship. Survivors were permitted to wear a gold-coloured torpedo sewn onto the left cuff of their jackets. A bar was added for each subsequent attack that was survived. These symbols of bravery were equivalent to the wound stripes awarded to men on the Western Front.

Walter Thorp is an example of a young man who had a remarkable wartime career: by the end of the war he had been torpedoed three times. He had joined the Merchant Navy in June 1914, just before the outbreak of war, and trained to be a 'Marconi man' (Chapter 59). Walter's role was to operate the Morse code device on ships. In the era before radio this was a vital way to send and receive information, and in particular to call for help if your ship was going down.

Walter's first brush with death came on 21 May 1917, aboard SS *City of Corinth*. This ship had almost completed a round trip from London to Singapore and back again, a distance of 19,000 nautical miles, when it was attacked within sight of Cornwall. U-boat *UB-31* sank the ship with a single torpedo but fortunately there were no casualties because the vessel sank so slowly. Walter stayed too long at his station sending out SOS messages and suddenly realised he was all alone. He waded through seawater to his cabin to rescue his pet canary in its wooden cage and together they abandoned ship. As they floated along together, the canary's singing kept Walter awake whenever he started to drift off – sleepiness being a sign of impending hypothermia.

On his next ship, SS *City of Cambridge*, Walter was attacked again – this time off the coast of Africa, near Algiers. U-boat *UC-67* fired the torpedo and, luckily, there was time once more to abandon ship without casualties. There was no canary to accompany him this time, but the

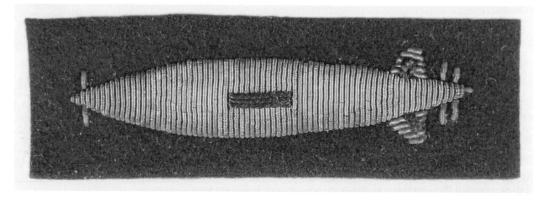

Walter Thorp, far right, with colleagues displaying his torpedo cuff badge with two bars.

floating survivors were worried by the appearance of sharks.

Walter's third and final shipwreck was on board SS *Mesaba* in September 1918. This time it was an even more frightening affair. About a day after departing Liverpool for Philadelphia, *Mesaba* was sunk in the Irish Sea by a torpedo from U-boat *UB-118*. It was a direct hit, and *Mesaba* went down so fast that twenty of Walter's crewmates died in the initial explosion or drowned as the ship slipped quickly beneath the waves.

Walter saw no further wartime action. He was not unique in surviving three shipwrecks during the First World War but it was a rarity. Given that around five thousand commercial ships were sunk during the conflict, it's a wonder that any Merchant Navy employee ever slept in their bunk at night while at sea.

77

Postcards of scuttled German warships at Scapa Flow

The single greatest loss of warships in history happened in the aftermath of the First World War

When the fighting ceased at the conclusion of the First World War, the ships of the Imperial German Navy were instructed to assemble off the east coast of Scotland. From here they were escorted to protected moorings at Scapa Flow in Orkney, while the peace talks continued in Paris. Part of these negotiations was to determine the eventual fate of the warships. Britain and the United States wanted them destroyed, but other allies wanted to divide them up between the victorious nations. There were eventually seventy-four impounded vessels including sixteen battleships and battlecruisers, the cream of the German High Seas Fleet.

While the talks continued, the Royal Navy was not permitted to board the ships except on official business and they remained assets of the German government. A reduced staff of German officers and ratings stayed behind, nominally in control of their vessels, but they were not allowed ashore and conditions on board soon became squalid and depressing.

The most senior naval officer present was Admiral Hans Hermann Ludwig von Reuter. He felt isolated because his government was not communicating with him, and soon became convinced that his ships were going to be surrendered. In his eyes this would be a shameful act, and he decided that he could not let it happen. There was usually a heavy Royal Navy presence, so Reuter bided his time.

The Admiral wrote to each vessel's commanding officer ordering all of them to prepare to scuttle their ships at his signal. On 21 June 1919 the Royal Navy took many of its ships out of Scapa Flow on military exercises. This was Reuter's opportunity. He sent the signal from his ship *Emden* using flags and lights, and his officers, who had had weeks to prepare, opened the seacocks and the water gushed in below decks.

It took some time for the message to reach the whole fleet because it was dispersed across a large area of Scapa Flow, yet one by one the German vessels started to disappear below the waves. Their crews abandoned ship in small open boats. The British servicemen at the naval base became flustered and did not know what to do initially. There were some regrettable incidents where unarmed German crewmen leaving their vessels were fired upon for committing what were seen as hostile acts. Nine were killed: the last German war casualties before the final peace was signed.

Gathering their wits, Royal Navy personnel sped to some of the sinking ships and managed to tow them into the shallows and beach them. In this way, they saved the battleship SMS *Baden* and twenty-one other ships. But a staggering fifty-two ships had been lost.

The British were furious and Reuter was imprisoned, although they were obliged to release him in early 1920. In Germany it was felt that he had salvaged a little honour after the fleet had been forced to surrender without a fight. In later years many of the wrecked vessels were refloated and salvaged for scrap.

78

Cecil Foster's best-selling book

A captain's account of the loss of SS Trevessa *in 1923: the biggest news story of that year*

The survival of the crew of SS *Trevessa* is an extraordinary tale of endurance at sea, and the captain's published account of events entitled *1700 miles in Open Boats* was an immediate bestseller.

In May 1923 *Trevessa* left Fremantle in Australia with a cargo of concentrated zinc ore. On 3 June the vessel ran into a storm and began taking on water. The ship's pumps were useless because the water entering the hold mixed with the cargo, turning it into a slurry. As water levels rose, *Trevessa* began to sink by the bows, so that on 4 June Captain Cecil Foster had no choice but to abandon ship in the middle of a vast expanse of ocean. All forty-four crewmen calmly left the ship in two small lifeboats, and managed to sit out the furious storm with its 30 foot waves and winds of 50mph.

Captain Foster had previously survived ten days at sea in an open boat after being torpedoed

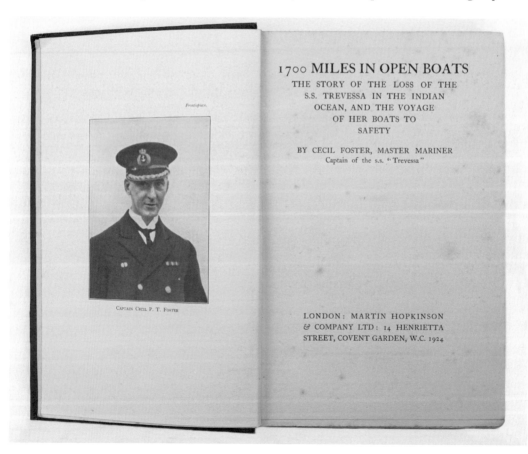

Frontispiece.

Captain Cecil P. T. Foster

1700 **MILES IN OPEN BOATS**

THE STORY OF THE LOSS OF THE
S.S. TREVESSA IN THE INDIAN
OCEAN, AND THE VOYAGE
OF HER BOATS TO
SAFETY

BY CECIL FOSTER, MASTER MARINER
Captain of the s.s. "Trevessa"

LONDON: MARTIN HOPKINSON
& COMPANY LTD: 14 HENRIETTA
STREET, COVENT GARDEN, W.C. 1924

in the First World War. This meant that he knew about the difficulties of sustaining life and morale. He and the first officer, James Smith, decided to make for the island of Rodriguez, which was 1,728 miles away, using sextants and compass to gauge direction. Foster calculated that rations would have to be stretched thinly if they were to make it: each man was permitted one biscuit per day, eight teaspoonfuls of condensed milk, and three tablespoons of water. Occasional rain was a real blessing.

Although initially together, the two boats soon separated: one commanded by Foster, the other by Smith. They used a sail whenever they could, but sometimes the men had to row. Foster's boat also leaked so had to be continually bailed out. In the end Foster's boat reached Rodriguez on 26 June, having lost only two men. Smith's boat missed Rodriguez but reached Mauritius three days later. Unfortunately, the crew on this boat fared less well: one man fell overboard; seven died from exposure, exhaustion or drinking seawater; and another man died shortly after reaching land. However, amazingly, thirty-three of the original crew had survived.

Ships that had responded to *Trevessa*'s original SOS found no survivors and concluded that everyone on board had perished. The crew's unexpected survival was an enormous relief to their families.

Cecil Foster and James Smith were widely praised for their abilities as seamen and leaders. They were interviewed by the press, filmed for the news, awarded the Lloyd's Medal for Saving Life at Sea, and even invited to an audience with King George V at Buckingham Palace. Foster's lifeboat was a star attraction at the British Empire Exhibition at Wembley in 1924–25.

Sadly, their improbable endurance against the odds perhaps took its toll on Captain Foster, who died a few years later in 1930, aged just 43.

All the survivors after a thanksgiving service on Mauritius.

Foster, his wife Minnie, and first officer James Smith, after meeting the King.

The lifeboat commanded by Captain Foster at the British Empire Exhibition.

Photo on the deck as a ship is sinking

A litany of incompetence and neglected safety killed 111 people on SS Vestris in 1928

The remarkable photograph overleaf was taken by crewmember Fred Hanson on 12 November 1928 as desperate preparations were being made to abandon ship. The passenger in the foreground, wearing a lifebelt, is bracing himself to stay upright as the stricken *Vestris* is listing heavily. Behind him, crewmen and passengers are lowering lifeboats.

Vestris sailed from New York on 10 November bound for Barbados and Buenos Aires, carrying 129 passengers and a crew of 197. It ran into heavy weather and began to list, and soon it became impossible to set the ship on an even keel. After prevaricating for far too long, the captain, William Carey, eventually ordered that SOS messages be sent out. Passengers and crew began to take to the lifeboats but it was badly organised, the sloping decks hampered everything, and in the middle of it all *Vestris* suddenly capsized. A recently launched lifeboat was smashed by one of the ship's cranes falling on it, killing everyone on board. Another sank because it was overloaded.

The human survivors and, bizarrely, the intrepid ship's cat, dispersed in various open boats and were picked up by four different rescue vessels after fourteen hours. These ships had been a long way away and *Vestris* had given out a location that was wrong by about 40 miles. A total of sixty-eight passengers and forty-three crew died, including all thirteen children on board and most of the women. Amongst the dead was Captain Carey.

Initially the press were told that a shifting cargo broke through bulkheads below decks in the storm and caused the list. However, *Vestris* had actually left New York in an unfit state, overladen beyond the safety limit, and already suffering from a slight list. *Vestris* had been reproached for this before.

In the storm the ship's list was made worse by water finding its way in through various hatches, doors and scuppers. This happened because the ship was sitting too low in the water to begin with, but also because the crew did not recognise and deal with the problem. There were suggestions that poor maintenance and design features were contributory factors.

The evacuation of the ship had been slow, lifeboat launching chaotic, and the ship's officers and crew were criticised for their incompetence. Furthermore, the ship's lifevests were an antiquated type that had been discontinued years before.

This disaster helped to formulate the international convention for the Safety Of Life At Sea (SOLAS) in 1929. It set international standards for lifevests, and improved evacuation procedures. Amongst its other provisions, it became mandatory for passenger ships and larger cargo ships to carry radio. During the sinking of *Vestris* there was another ship just 6 miles away but neither knew of the other's existence because the second ship did not have radio. Every life could have been saved.

Ironically, twenty-five British survivors were taken home on SS *Celtic*, which, when almost home, was itself wrecked off the coast of Ireland, mercifully without further deaths.

The ill-fated *Vestris* – passengers donning outmoded lifevests.

80

Unmarked grave of Arthur John Priest

Survivor of an astonishing four shipwrecks, who died in 1937

Hollybrook Cemetery in Southampton holds the graves of many seafarers, but perhaps none more remarkable than Arthur John Priest.

Priest worked for the Merchant Navy, and his first brush with death came on board *Titanic*'s sister ship, RMS *Olympic*, which collided with HMS *Hawke* in 1911. Happily, although *Olympic* suffered serious damage, it did not sink.

However, the following year, aged 25, he signed up to join *Titanic*. He was paid £6 a month as a fireman, a role which in navy parlance was termed a stoker. He probably considered himself fortunate to get a job because lots of men were being laid off at the time. After the ship hit the iceberg, Priest raced up on deck. It was a long way from the engine room in the bowels of the ship to the main deck, so when he reached there

the lifeboats had all gone. Priest had no choice but to dive overboard and swim for it in the freezing waters of the Atlantic. Luckily, he was picked up by a lifeboat and survived.

When the First World War started, Priest supported the war effort in his role as a Merchant Navy fireman. In early 1916 he was aboard *Alcantara*, a former passenger liner converted to an armed merchant cruiser. The vessel was attacked by the German raider SMS *Greif* and after a short, intense battle at close quarters, both ships went to the bottom. Over seventy members of *Alcantara*'s crew died, but Priest again was one of the fortunate ones.

His next close shave came in November 1916 whilst on another White Star liner, *Britannic*, which was acting as a hospital ship. He was in good company on board this vessel because *Titanic* survivors Violet Jessop and Archie Jewell were also on board. The liner struck a mine off the coast of Greece and sank. Many people jumped into the water, including Priest, who was pulled right under the still-rotating propeller and, in his own words, he 'said goodbye to the world'. Yet, miraculously, a large piece of wood saved him from being sliced apart and he resurfaced in safety. He and the other ex-*Titanic* crewmembers all escaped once more.

Finally in 1917 he was serving as fireman on *Donegal*, another hospital ship, when it was torpedoed by a U-boat in the English Channel. Forty wounded soldiers and members of the crew died, but Priest got away yet again. Unfortunately, his crew mate and co-survivor from *Titanic*, Archie Jewell, did not make it this time.

Priest earned the nickname of the 'unsinkable stoker', and once said that men refused to serve with him because he was considered unlucky. This may be why he ended his seagoing career prematurely. He died of pneumonia at home in 1937, aged just 49, and it seems a pity that at the conclusion of such an extraordinary life there should be no gravestone to commemorate one of the UK's greatest shipwreck survivors.

Souvenir badge for passengers

TSS Athenia *was the first British ship sunk in the Second World War*

*A*thenia was a popular passenger liner, and enamelled badges were amongst a number of souvenirs available to purchase on board. The badge depicts the house flag of the owners, the Donaldson Line, with the vessel's name on a ship's wheel. *Athenia* was a turbine steam ship, hence the prefix letters TSS. The ship departed Glasgow on 1 September 1939, bound ultimately for Montreal. On board were in excess of 1,400 people including Jewish refugees, American and Canadian citizens heading home to avoid the impending war, and a crew of around 300. Approximately three-quarters of the passengers were women and children.

On 3 September Prime Minister Neville Chamberlain addressed the nation on the radio. A little after 11am he declared 'this country

is at war with Germany'. Later the same day, at 7.38pm, U-boat *U-30* fired a torpedo at SS *Athenia*, without warning, which was to send it to the bottom of the Atlantic. *Athenia* was, of course, completely unarmed and the U-boat attack was in contravention of international law. Although the ship did not sink until the next morning, more than a hundred people died. Crewmen were killed in the engine room where the torpedo hit and, sadly, most passengers died when two lifeboats were destroyed by accident in the haste to abandon ship. Six ships were involved in the rescue, all of them wary of being attacked themselves.

Passenger Elisabeth Turner recalled: 'Suddenly there was a terrific explosion, and I was thrown to the deck. I reckon I must be the luckiest woman on earth, as when I recovered from the shock I saw several men lying dead on the deck quite near me . . . The lifeboat into which I was put capsized, but was righted again and all the people managed to get back again.'

The incident provoked international outrage, and was instantly compared to the German sinking of *Lusitania* twenty-five years before. As on that previous occasion, the Germans were afraid that their ill-judged attack on an unarmed passenger ship would bring the United States into the war. Consequently, the Nazis refused to admit culpability and, bizarrely, promoted a ludicrous conspiracy theory that Winston Churchill had ordered the sinking of *Athenia* to provoke American involvement in the war effort.

A confession of guilt did not emerge until the Nuremberg Trials in 1946, where Nazis were tried for war crimes. An admission was made that the commander of *U-30*, Fritz Julius Lemp, had followed *Athenia* for some time before coming to the erroneous conclusion that it was an armed British vessel because of its dark paint and evasive zig-zag course. He fired two torpedoes, one of which missed. When he realised what he had done he later falsified the U-boat's log, and Nazi leaders were afraid to admit responsibility.

U-boat *U-30* returning to port; Fritz Julius Lemp is standing in the conning tower.

82

Lifeboat from SS Anglo-Saxon

*The craft that enabled two young men to survive adrift in the
Atlantic for a formidable seventy days*

Robert Tapscott, aged 19, and Roy Widdicombe, 21, were both on the crew of the unescorted British freighter SS *Anglo-Saxon* in 1940. One night, a few hundred miles west of the Azores, the German raider *Widder* attacked their ship and sank it. The crew were taken completely by surprise, and the first wave of shells destroyed their radio so they could alert no one to their plight. Seven of the forty or so crew managed to escape in the ship's 18-foot jolly-boat before the freighter went down. Agonisingly, they drifted right across the bows of their attacker, but *Widder* was so intent on finishing off *Anglo-Saxon* that they went unnoticed in the darkness. No one dared move in case they drew attention to themselves. Shortly afterwards they watched in horror as other crewmates who had escaped on liferafts were spotted by the enemy and callously machine-gunned to death.

Anglo-Saxon went to the bottom and the raider vanished. Next morning Tapscott, Widdicombe and the other survivors were alone in a great expanse of blue. They had some food and water, tobacco and a compass, and hoped to be picked up soon. They narrowly dodged a German ship

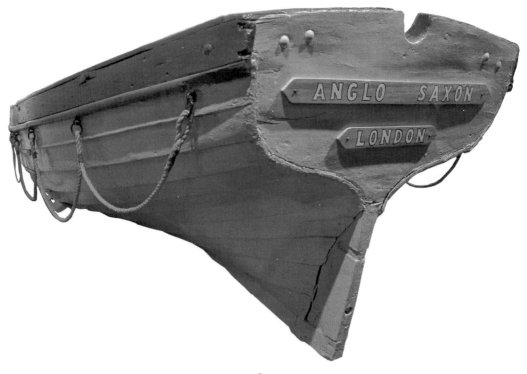

at night, but it was baking hot during the day and they soon exhausted their meagre supply of water.

One injured man died of gangrene, and another, who knew he was dying of the same cause, threw himself overboard. The remainder endured as best they could, but the thirst, heat and despair at not being rescued took their toll. The third engineer and the mate agreed a suicide pact and dived over the side together, followed a few days later by the second cook.

Tapscott and Widdicombe were the last two men left alive; both considered suicide but never gave in to it. They were badly burned by the sun and survived on rainwater, seaweed and a few fish. One day they saw a passenger liner and waved to it frantically, but it steamed past them; they also had to contend with a fearsome storm.

Incredibly, the duo endured seventy days at sea and completed a 2,300-mile journey to the Bahamas, where, little more than skin and bone, they were found exhausted on a beach by islanders. They had each lost almost half their bodyweight. They made a full recovery in hospital.

Life seems to treat some people very unfairly, and poor Widdicombe, having lived through so much, was killed on his way home when his ship was sunk by a U-boat. Tapscott did make it home and testified against Ruchteschell, the commander of the U-boat who had machine-gunned the *Anglo-Saxon*'s liferafts. The German was sentenced as a war criminal and died in prison. Tapscott married and had a daughter, but perhaps never fully recovered from his ordeal and sadly committed suicide in 1963, aged 42.

Robert Tapscott (left) and Roy Widdicombe (right).

83

Memorial plaque on Merseyside

Commemorating Britain's worst ever shipping disaster

There are many maritime memorials in Liverpool, but this small plaque helps to ensure that the appalling tragedy of RMS *Lancastria* is never forgotten. Having said this, the disaster is unfamiliar to many because of the limited media attention it received.

Lancastria was a Cunard ship requisitioned as a troopship. In June 1940, shortly after the main evacuation of British forces from Dunkirk, *Lancastria* sailed to France for Operation Aerial to rescue remaining Allied civilians and military personnel. On 17 June it was moored off St Nazaire and thousands of individuals were ferried aboard. The precise figure will never be known because the mass of people desperate to escape made it impossible to keep track of them all. This ship was built to carry 2,200 passengers but the captain, Rudolph Sharp, was told to take as many people as possible, regardless of laws or safety regulations. When it was ready to sail, there were at least five thousand people on board and maybe as many as nine thousand.

Lancastria was a passenger liner: it was not designed to withstand enemy fire. Despite the need to avoid being attacked, *Lancastria* waited for other ships to complete their embarkations so that they could leave together under escort to protect them from U-boats. Sadly, this was to prove a fatal delay. Enemy aircraft had been seen dropping bombs in their vicinity earlier

HMT LANCASTRIA

The Lancastria was sunk by enemy action near the French port of St Nazaire whilst evacuating British servicemen, crew and civilians on the

17th June 1940

Considered to be the worst disaster in British maritime history. There were just 2,477 survivors. It is thought that as many as 6,000 people lost their lives.

WE WILL REMEMBER THEM

Oh hear us when we cry to Thee, for those in peril on the sea

in the afternoon, and at 1.48pm the nearby SS *Oronsay* was hit, yet still *Lancastria* waited. It was an anxious time.

At 3.48pm a Junkers 88 bomber lined up *Lancastria* in its sights and four bombs hit the unmoving over-crowded ship. It was a sitting duck. The bombs went through the upper deck and exploded deep in the vessel amongst the evacuees and crew. It was a massacre. The ship sank in about twenty minutes. A few lifeboats were launched, but people thrown overboard or who jumped into the sea found themselves struggling in oil from ruptured fuel tanks. To make matters worse, some were cruelly machine-gunned from the air. Some survivors fought each other for lifebelts. Many spent hours in the water.

The number of dead remains unknown. It is commonly estimated at four thousand but may have been far more. To put this horrendous total into perspective, the combined loss of life from *Titanic* (Chapter 63), *Lusitania* (Chapter 68) and *Empress of Ireland* (Chapter 66) amounts to about 3,715 people.

The government had recently announced the morale-sapping Dunkirk evacuations, and France ceased hostilities against the Germans on 17 June, heralding the imminent French surrender. Churchill decided that adding the destruction of *Lancastria* would be too much for the public. He embargoed all news related to *Lancastria* by slapping a D-notice on all media coverage. This is perhaps the major reason why this horrific event is not better known.

Promotional image for *Lancastria* from the 1930s.

84

Book of remembrance

Part of the memorial to HMS Hood *in a New Forest church*

My father was 12 years old when HMS *Hood* was sunk. He told me how his own father had come home one day looking very grave and announced in a quiet yet emotional voice: 'They've sunk the *Hood*.' It was Britain's most prestigious warship, and the impact on morale in 1941 was profound.

Hood had been sent out as part of a squadron to intercept the powerful German ships *Bismarck* and *Prinz Eugen*, which were heading for the Atlantic intent on destroying Allied convoys. This could not be allowed to happen. Merchant ships bringing troops and vital supplies from North America were already highly vulnerable to U-boats and the Royal Navy's convoy escort ships would have been no match for the two mighty German vessels.

Vice Admiral Lancelot Holland was in overall command of the initiative, and *Hood* was his flagship. Early in the morning on 24 May 1941,

IN MEMORY OF
VICE-ADMIRAL · LANCELOT · ERNEST · HOLLAND · C.B.
AND 1416 OFFICERS AND MEN OF H.M.S. HOOD
KILLED IN ACTION 24TH MAY 1941

TRANQUIL THEY LIE
THEY DARED BOLDLY IN A FAIR CAUSE

in the Denmark Strait, the German battleships were sighted. The vessels opened fire, and shortly after the engagement began, at about 6am, shells from *Bismarck* struck *Hood* near the mainmast. There was a sudden, massive explosion and to the consternation of everyone present *Hood* sank stern first within three minutes. It had been a lucky hit, somehow exploiting a weakness that detonated the ship's magazine. The exact reason for the explosion has been debated, but may never now be determined: when the wreck was located in 2001, the relevant parts of the ship had been destroyed.

Only three of the ship's crew survived, picked up two hours later by HMS *Electra*; in total, 1,415 men died. It was the greatest loss of life on a British warship in history. Seventy-one of the lost crew were only 16 or 17 years of age.

Despite this appalling blow, the British were still faced with the problem of *Bismarck* potentially running riot through its vital convoys. It was an issue that could not be ignored. Churchill was all too aware of it and almost immediately issued the famous order to the Royal Navy: 'Sink the Bismarck.' The German ship was pursued relentlessly and just three days later, on 27 May, it was destroyed.

The book of remembrance lists everyone who died on *Hood*, and was the inspiration of Vice Admiral Holland's widow, Phyllis. There were no plans for a national memorial

to the ship after the war, despite the heavy death toll. Yet Mrs Holland determined to create one at the local church where she and her husband had worshipped: St John's Church, Boldre, in the New Forest. Apart from the book of remembrance, other items at the church include a stained glass window, two benches carved with *Hood*'s badge, and an original painting of the ship. An official commemoration service is held at the church every year.

Beautifully carved ship's badge on a bench at St John's Church, Boldre.

85

Doris Hawkins' remarkable account

A story showing the unexpected humanity of an enemy but the inhumanity of an ally

On 12 September 1942 Doris Hawkins, a nurse on RMS *Laconia*, returned to her quarters after dinner. On board were Allied military personnel and their families, and 1,800 Italian prisoners of war. While Doris was talking to a friend there were two explosions: Doris knew they had been torpedoed. She grabbed Sally, the baby she was responsible for, and joined the surge of people rushing towards the main deck. On the way, the lights failed and the ship began to list. Once on deck, every lifeboat seemed either full or broken. An RAF officer helped Doris to find a place on a lifeboat, but it capsized on launch. Doris lost hold of Sally and never saw her again.

People were thrashing in the water, but Doris reached a raft and watched *Laconia* sink. She and her compatriots were covered in fuel oil, and had swallowed some, which made them sick. They were cold and wet and had no provisions; one man on Doris's raft died of his wounds.

On their second night adrift, much to everyone's surprise, the U-boat that had sunk *Laconia* appeared, threw them a line, and took them on board. They were fed, treated, warmed and allowed to sleep. Doris said: 'the Germans treated us with great kindness and respect'. The U-boat's commanding officer, Werner Hartenstein, had taken pity on them. He radioed for assistance and garnered support from other U-boats. An Italian submarine arrived and took away Italian survivors, and Vichy France agreed to send ships to collect the others. Lifeboats and rafts were towed behind the U-boats, with some survivors still in them due to lack of space within the submarines.

The Germans' humanitarian rescue mission was interrupted by an American plane which bombed the U-boats despite them displaying red cross flags, towing boats of survivors and signalling their mission to the plane. The U-boats had no choice but to abandon the survivors, cut their boats free and dive. It was impossible for them to dive filled with survivors. Tactfully, in her wartime account, Doris does not identify that the Americans were responsible.

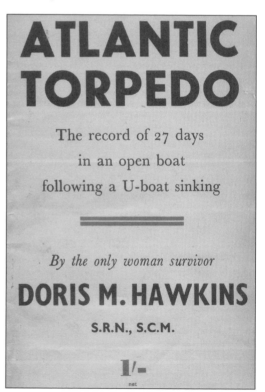

ATLANTIC TORPEDO

The record of 27 days
in an open boat
following a U-boat sinking

By the only woman survivor

DORIS M. HAWKINS

S.R.N., S.C.M.

1/-
net

RMS *Laconia* before the war.

The survivors had to swim to their lifeboats and many drowned. Doris found herself with one woman and sixty-six men crammed into a leaking 30-foot boat with no rudder that soon became separated from the other boats. They had two ounces of water each per day and very meagre rations. Soon they developed sores, infections, aches, sunburn and great weakness. One by one they died. At the end of their third week afloat they ran out of water but were saved by a timely six-hour deluge which topped up their reserves.

After twenty-seven days afloat they ran aground on the coast of Liberia. They crawled ashore and local people helped them. Only sixteen had survived, although one poor man died shortly afterwards of gangrene. Other survivors had been picked up by rescue ships, principally the French cruiser *Gloire*. In all, about 1,100 people survived *Laconia*'s sinking, but probably in excess of 1,600 died.

Doris eventually made it home to England, publishing her account in 1943. She survived the war.

86

Model of a Japanese bomber

During the Second World War ships were exposed to greater
aerial threats than ever before

Only a handful of naval vessels were sunk by aircraft in the First World War. A notable example was the submarine HMS *B10*, which was bombed by Austro-Hungarian planes at Venice. It was the first submarine in history to be sunk by aircraft, yet luckily there were no casualties.

Military aircraft were much more effective as an attacking option by the Second World War.

They could fly further, were faster, had greater manoeuvrability and were better armed. In particular, the attack on Pearl Harbor on 7 December 1941 revealed the potency of Japanese aircraft, which destroyed 188 American planes and killed 2,403 service personnel. USS *Arizona* was hit by a bomb, exploded and sank, killing 1,177 people. About eighteen other American ships were destroyed or damaged.

Three days later the Royal Navy lost HMS *Prince of Wales* and HMS *Repulse* to aerial attacks as they steamed towards Malaysia. These were the first capital ships in history to be sunk by aircraft in open water. The land-based Japanese aircraft dropped both bombs and torpedoes.

In the 1940s land-based aircraft could fly only a limited distance over water because otherwise they would run out of fuel, so the use of bombers from aircraft carriers became a significant threat to ocean shipping. The plane shown on the previous page is an Aichi D3A1 Type 99 dive-bomber, a type that operated from aircraft carriers. It was one of the aircraft used at Pearl Harbor but they soon targeted British ships as well.

On Easter Day 1942 the heavy cruisers HMS *Dorsetshire* and HMS *Cornwall* were at sea aiming to rejoin the Royal Navy fleet in the Indian Ocean. Unfortunately, they were spotted by a Japanese plane, and attacked by Type 99 dive-bombers despatched from enemy aircraft carriers. Each carried a single 250kg bomb under the main fuselage and a smaller bomb under each wing. The planes dived towards the ships at a steep angle, making it hard to destroy them with anti-aircraft fire, and then dropped their bombs from a low height to ensure accurate targeting.

Dorsetshire was hit repeatedly, quickly losing communications, power and steering. Further bombs started fires, exploded an ammunition magazine, ruptured the hull and damaged the engines. *Dorsetshire* began to list, and men jumped or were thrown overboard only to be machine-gunned in the water by passing planes. The ship turned over and went down within ten minutes. The dive-bombers dealt with *Cornwall* in a similar fashion and it foundered just a few minutes later.

The survivors of both ships were now in the open ocean, with a few boats between them, some floating debris to cling to, and limited provisions. Thick oil welled up to the surface from the wrecks, making life extremely unpleasant for those in the water. Officers managed to get their men together and, mercifully, they were picked up the next day – 1,122 men from both ships survived, but 424 had died.

87

Sailor's cap tally

The dramatic loss of HMS Curacoa *was kept secret because of the potential impact on wartime morale*

A tally is a ribbon bearing a ship's name that sailors in the Royal Navy tie around their caps. They have traditionally been black with gold lettering. The fate of many men sporting this particular tally in the Second World War is both astonishing and distressing.

Curacoa was an elderly cruiser that was allocated to convoy protection duties for most of the Second World War. On 2 October 1942, under Captain John Boutwood, *Curacoa* was assigned to meet the liner RMS *Queen Mary* off the coast of Ireland and escort it safely to Greenock. *Queen Mary* was carrying around ten thousand American troops and the ship's commodore, Sir Cyril Illingworth, was under orders not to stop for any reason. *Queen Mary* was a very fast ship that could outrun U-boats, but if it stopped it would be a sitting target and with so many troops on board the consequences of a torpedo attack were unthinkable.

As was common practice, both ships pursued a fast zig-zag course to make it difficult for U-boats to target them. However, the two captains had different ideas about which vessel had right of way. This meant that when their two courses intersected, both believed the other ship would alter course. By the time that collision was inevitable, it was too late to take

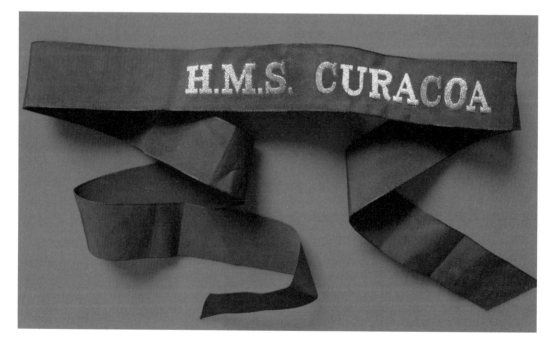

HMS *Curacoa* at sea.

evasive action. The result was that *Queen Mary* hit HMS *Curacoa* amidships at full speed – about 25 knots – and simply cut it in half. Alfred Johnson, a seaman on the ocean liner, said his ship 'sliced the cruiser in two like a piece of butter, straight through the six inch armoured plating'.

The naval vessel's stern section sank immediately, but the remainder stayed afloat for a few minutes. Under orders not to stop, *Queen Mary*'s crew watched helplessly as their ship steamed ahead regardless, leaving the *Curacoa*'s crew to their fate. They radioed the more distant warships on convoy duty and requested assistance, but it was some hours before the survivors were picked up. In all, about one hundred men were rescued, including Captain Boutwood, but 337 were killed.

This tragedy was hushed up during the war and those who had witnessed the event were told to stay quiet. The disaster was only revealed to the public after the conclusion of hostilities, and there was shock at the scale of the death toll as well as great sadness for the families who had lost men in an incident that should have been completely avoidable.

In the meantime the Admiralty sought legal redress from Cunard White Star Line, the owners of *Queen Mary*. An initial ruling found *Curacoa*'s officers entirely at fault, but on appeal the blame was established as two-thirds Admiralty, and one-third the shipping line.

88

HMS Belfast

A ship that was nearly wrecked itself helped to destroy a notorious enemy battlecruiser

If one word sums up HMS *Belfast*, perhaps it is 'survivor'. The ship was nearly lost in 1939 after hitting a mine and the damage was so extensive that it took three years to return to service. Subsequently, *Belfast* protected Allied shipping in convoys, helped sink an infamous battlecruiser, and took part in the D-Day landings. Having endured the Second World War and then the Korean War, it lives on still, moored on the Thames near Tower Bridge where it has been preserved as a unique museum ship since 1971.

The losses of merchant shipping to German U-boats reached staggering proportions in the Second World War, and naval escort vessels were vital to reducing the losses. *Belfast* was a powerful ship, and operated on the Arctic convoys – ensuring that vital supplies reached Britain's wartime ally, the Soviet Union. The conditions were punishing, with bitter cold and ice to contend with, as well as the constant threat of enemy attack from beneath the freezing surface of the sea. *Belfast*'s sister ship, HMS *Edinburgh*, was sunk by the enemy while escorting Arctic convoys.

In 1943 intercepted communications revealed that a fleet of German ships had left their base in Norway, planning to strike a convoy. The enemy flagship was the formidable battlecruiser *Scharnhorst*, one of the most threatening ships afloat. It had long posed a menace and the Admiralty was keen to deal with it once and for all.

The plan was for Admiral Robert Burnett in *Belfast*, accompanied by HMS *Norfolk* and *Sheffield*, to protect the convoy, while Admiral Bruce Fraser in HMS *Duke of York* supported by several other ships would cut off *Scharnhorst*'s retreat to Norway. This would force the engagement that has become known as the Battle of North Cape.

Scharnhorst's escort ships were ordered away and the imposing battlecruiser steamed on alone. *Belfast* soon located the enemy on radar, and the closer *Norfolk* opened fire. By chance, this disabled the radar that enabled accurate targeting of its shells, but *Scharnhorst* returned fire and continued to pursue the convoy regardless. Soon *Belfast*, *Norfolk* and *Sheffield* were all firing at the enemy, which had reduced ability to hit its British attackers and so turned back to Norway. By now, Admiral Fraser and his fleet were in position. In the chase that followed, *Belfast* fired illuminated flares to light up *Scharnhorst* so that *Duke of York* and its compatriots could strike.

A brutal assault with shells and then torpedoes followed, with the German rear admiral vowing to fight until his last shell. The British ships systematically finished off the battlecruiser. The wreck of the once-mighty *Scharnhorst* sank like a stone in the icy Arctic waters, exploding beneath the waves, and taking 1,927 German crewmen to their deaths. A mere thirty-six were rescued.

It ranks as one of the greatest losses of life in a shipwreck, and marks the last ever ship-to-ship battle in European waters.

89

MRC War Memorandum No. 8

Official advice on the care of shipwrecked people during the Second World War

The Medical Research Council issued a number of wartime memoranda on subjects such as emergency amputations and preventing hospital infections. War Memorandum No. 8 in 1943 was concerned with preserving life at sea after shipwreck.

Given that thousands of British and Allied ships had already been lost by 1943, it is a wonder that national advice was not published much earlier. Besides being not very timely, the report, discouragingly, starts by quoting extensively from a book published in the time of Nelson! The report was aimed mainly at seafarers who escaped a sinking ship via lifeboats. The advice represented the 'pooled knowledge of sailors and scientists' and was commended to Royal Navy and Merchant Navy officers, nautical schools and medical officers. The authors stressed that nearly half of all lifeboats adrift for more than twenty-four hours reached safety within five days, and that the leadership and conduct of the officer in charge was one of the most important factors affecting a positive outcome.

Crews were advised to adopt routines at sea which maximised survival chances should their ship be attacked. This included checking lifeboats regularly, always sleeping fully clothed in case their vessel sank suddenly, and memorising the ship's position every day. Once in a lifeboat there were suggestions on how to behave: 'Do not exhaust yourself by getting excited. Do not sing or shout: for by so doing you use up your strength and lose valuable water in your breath.' It was recommended that everyone in a lifeboat be given a job to do, no matter how small.

Practical advice was also given about protection from the elements, rationing of water, and first aid. Common medical complaints in a drifting lifeboat included dry mouth, cracked skin, salt-water burns, inflammation of the eyes, bowel upsets, swollen legs due to immobility, frostbite and 'immersion foot' caused by prolonged soaking of the legs. Survivors were instructed not to drink seawater or their own urine, and were told that although sharks were not as dangerous as commonly believed, mirages could be a significant concern.

Lifeboat first aid kits contained amphetamine tablets, which could 'lessen feelings of fatigue and exhaustion, promote alertness, raise the spirits, and prolong the will to "hang on" and live'. They were recommended to keep look-outs awake, counter severe exhaustion or when a special effort was needed, such as a spell of hard rowing.

Finally, guidance was given on maximising the chance of rescue by maintaining a look-out, applying principles of good navigation, and outlining methods of attracting attention from potential rescuers.

M.R.C. War Memorandum No. 8

Medical Research Council:
Committee on the Care of
Shipwrecked Personnel

A GUIDE TO
THE PRESERVATION OF LIFE
AT SEA AFTER SHIPWRECK

LONDON
PUBLISHED BY HIS MAJESTY'S STATIONERY OFFICE
To be purchased directly from H.M. STATIONERY OFFICE at the following addresses:
York House, Kingsway, London, W.C.2; 120 George Street, Edinburgh 2;
39-41 King Street, Manchester 2; 1 St. Andrew's Crescent, Cardiff;
80 Chichester Street, Belfast;
or through any bookseller

1943

Price 4d. net

90

A ship's log on sailcloth

Kept by a survivor of SS Lulworth Hill *after being torpedoed*

Compared to German U-boats, Italian submarines had much more limited impact during the Second World War. The most successful was *Leonardo da Vinci*, commanded by Gianfranco Gazzana-Priaroggia, which sank seventeen Allied ships. Its final patrol began with the sinking of RMS *Empress of Canada* on 19 March 1943 – which ironically was transporting Italian prisoners of war – followed by six other ships.

Leonardo da Vinci's second target was the British cargo ship SS *Lulworth Hill*. This vessel had a crew of over forty-five and was torpedoed at night off the west coast of Africa, where it sank quickly. Ship's carpenter Kenneth Cooke jumped overboard, and swam through oil and debris until at daybreak he spotted a life-raft. He reached it, exhausted, and was helped aboard by another survivor. Together they searched for others, and eventually fourteen men occupied the raft; several were only teenagers.

The raft was 10 feet by 8, with meagre provisions. Men were allowed two ounces of water (about 60ml) three times per day, plus two or three dried milk tablets for breakfast, a spoonful of fish paste for lunch and two pieces of chocolate at tea-time.

Sharks were a constant threat and had eaten men in the water immediately after the ship went down. They circled the survivors constantly: some were almost twice the length of the raft. The largest was nicknamed 'Scarface'.

Cooke created the log shown opposite, using a pencil to write on strips of sailcloth. He recorded the fate of *Lulworth Hill*, the names of the survivors and what happened to them. They drifted towards the equator, becoming weaker in the blazing 38°C heat. On 6 April, after eighteen days afloat, the first man died – the chief officer, Basil Scown, leaving Cooke in command. The death devastated their morale and, within ten days, five other men had died. Each body had to be put over the side where the sharks devoured them. It must have been horrendous to realise that you might be next.

The survivors were emaciated, sunburned and desperately thirsty. A few became delirious, sometimes exacerbated by drinking seawater. One man suddenly leapt up and dragged two others over the side with him. Cooke ordered that the ill man be left to the sharks as he was a danger to the rest. Only one of the other men was able to clamber back on board; the other was killed by sharks.

After five weeks there were only two men left alive – Cooke and seaman Colin Armitage. They considered suicide, but didn't go through with it. Towards the end they had only two ounces of water each per day. Eventually they were spotted by a plane, and five days later were picked up by HMS *Rapid*. By some miracle they had survived fifty harrowing days on the ocean. Their families had long since been told that they were dead.

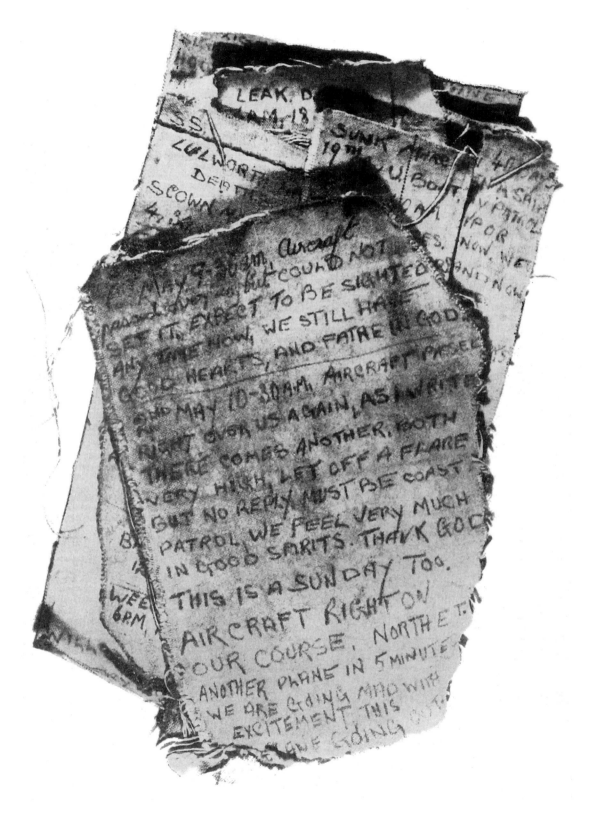

91

Snapshots of ships aground

SS Leicester *was the ship that would not sink, snapped by a holidaymaker in 1948*

There are many tales of sailors who have been shipwrecked several times, but not many stories of ships that have been given up for lost on more than one occasion.

SS *Leicester* was a cargo vessel built originally in the USA as *Samesk* in 1944 to aid the war effort. *Samesk* made it through the conflict unscathed, and after the war was taken over by the Federal Steam Navigation Company and renamed *Leicester*. In September 1948 the ship left Tilbury in Essex with a cargo of gravel bound for New York. All went well until 14 September, when *Leicester* was about 700 miles northeast of Bermuda. Here the ship was repeatedly hit by huge waves generated by Hurricane VII from the Caribbean.

The gravel cargo shifted en masse in the heavy seas and caused the ship to list to port – initially a 30 degree list, later progressively increasing to a staggering 70 degrees. Unsurprisingly, the crew decided to abandon ship, and most were rescued by a passing vessel, although six crewmen died during the difficult evacuation.

It was feared that *Leicester* was lost, of course, but nonetheless two salvage tugs, *Foundation Josephine* and *Foundation Lillian*, were sent out to search for the vessel and they eventually found it, taking the stricken ship in tow. Towing proved extraordinarily difficult due to the list and the fact that *Leicester*'s rudder had jammed, which made the ship continually sheer sideways.

On 3 October the tugs delivered their prize to the normally safe haven of Murray's Anchorage at Bermuda. Work quickly began to shift the gravel cargo so that the ship would float on an even keel. Yet this task had not been completed before another Caribbean hurricane blew up. Hurricane VIII battered the island and both *Leicester* and the salvage tug *Josephine* were driven ashore, as the photos opposite show. *Leicester* had been secured by around 30 tons of mooring anchors but still ended up hard aground on the rocks and had to be rescued again. It took some time.

Eventually *Leicester* was towed to New York to complete her original voyage, and was repaired. The ship was sold several times and changed its name to *Inagua*, then *Serafin Topic*, then *Jela Topic* and finally *Viking Liberty*. Under this last name, the ship ran aground at Trinidad in January 1966 and repairs were not deemed economic so the vessel was broken up for scrap. Third time unlucky: but at last poor *Leicester* could rest in peace.

92

Sailors' Church, Liverpool

*Rebuilt in 1952 after war damage, it has long offered comfort
to seafarers and their families*

There are many buildings in the UK that have been known as the 'sailors' church', but arguably the Church of Our Lady and Saint Nicholas in Liverpool is the best known. There has been a place of worship on this site since medieval times, but the body of the church was demolished by enemy bombing in the Second World War and rebuilt in 1952. The tower is older and dates back to the early nineteenth century.

This church has long been associated with St Nicholas, the patron saint of seafarers, and local people went there for centuries to pray for the safe return of family members. The hazards of shipwreck were all too common and, besides prayer, divine protection might also be urged by presenting small offerings to the saint. Nicholas is supposed to have been a bishop in the city of Myra in modern Turkey. Amongst other miracles he is said to have caused a fearsome storm to subside while he was on a ship at sea, simply by reprimanding the elements. Accordingly, there is a stained glass window in Liverpool's church depicting St Nicholas carefully cradling a modern ship as if to safeguard it from harm.

The association of religion and protection from the sea goes back many millennia. The ancient Greeks asked for blessings from Poseidon, the god of the sea, before embarking on voyages and the Romans sought protection from their equivalent deity, Neptune.

Sometimes coastal Christian communities in the UK adopted pagan-style approaches to maritime safety, such as 'blessing the sea' ceremonies. These were often colourful events, typically featuring a procession followed by a church service conducted near the shore. There were traditionally prayers for the safety of seafarers and local boats, and the sea itself might be blessed by the sprinkling of holy water. Although more popular in the past, these ceremonies still occur in some locations especially, it seems, in southeast England at places such as Hastings and Folkestone.

In Victorian times the Church had an important role in the event of any major disaster by offering solace and reassurance. Shipwrecks often occasioned memorial services, and sermons were published for national consumption after a significant loss of life. A major theme of religious discourse related to shipwrecks was that Christians needed to keep their faith in God even when sorely tested by imminent death. Reports of passengers praying together calmly till the bitter end were widely eulogised, although one suspects that such accounts were often sanitised by survivors to comfort family members of the victims. It was reported with a sense of pride that the band on the deck of *Titanic* supposedly played *Nearer My God to Thee* during the great liner's final minutes.

Right: St Nicholas holds a ship protectively in a window of the Liverpool church.

Below: A 'blessing the sea' ceremony in Hastings in 1904.

93

Tower Hill memorial

Completed in 1955, the memorial honours Merchant Navy crews from both world wars who have no grave but the sea

The statistics for ships and personnel lost in the two world wars is both staggering and sobering. According to the Commonwealth War Graves Commission, 3,305 Merchant Navy and fishing vessels were lost in the First World War, together with 17,000 lives. The peak came in 1917, when the Germans launched 'unrestricted submarine warfare', but the adoption of the Royal Navy convoy escort system subsequently turned the tide against the U-boats and significantly reduced losses.

In the Second World War the toll was even higher: 4,786 merchant ships and 32,000 lives

lost, with 1942 representing the peak year and U-boats again being the principal cause of destruction. The Atlantic witnessed the greatest losses because North America was the most important source of troops, military equipment, supplies, food and raw materials for the Allied war effort. However, there were significant losses on the Arctic convoys to Russia as well, and in ships operating in the Mediterranean.

The Tower Hill Memorial near the Tower of London honours Merchant Navy personnel of all ranks whose bodies were never found. It was completed in two parts. The First World

War commemoration identifies about twelve thousand casualties with no grave but the sea, named on bronze plaques in a large roofed colonnade resembling a mausoleum. There was initial wrangling about the form it should take and its location, with a more prominent site next to the Thames being rejected. It was designed by Sir Edwin Lutyens, who was also responsible for the Cenotaph on Whitehall, amongst many other memorials, and the sculptor was Sir William Reid-Dick. The memorial was unveiled by Queen Mary, wife of George V, on 12 December 1928.

The memorial was extended after the Second World War to identify about twenty-four thousand men who died and whose bodies were never found. It takes the form of a semi-circular sunken garden, with its entrance heralded by two stone pylons that face the First World War memorial. Each pylon bears an equally large figure: a Merchant Navy seaman on one side, and an officer on the other – helping perhaps to convey the message that rank and social status become irrelevant in death. This newer section was designed by Sir Edward Maufe, with sculpture by Charles Wheeler, and Queen Elizabeth II unveiled it on 5 November 1955.

A smaller memorial to the Merchant Navy personnel who died in the Falklands War (1982) was added in 2005. It takes the form of a sundial.

A Merchant Navy officer guarding the entrance to the Second World War memorial.

Some of the thousands of names commemorated.

94

A dead seabird

Much wildlife was killed when Torrey Canyon *broke apart in 1967*

The environmental impact of shipwrecks can be significant. The wrecks of ships from many decades ago gradually leak their oil fuel into the oceans as their hulls rust under the water, and it then enters the food chain. However, some of the most acute impacts on marine life result from the loss of bulk tankers transporting oil because the quantities released into the sea can be vast.

In 1967 *Torrey Canyon* was transporting about 120,000 tons of oil from Kuwait to refineries at Milford Haven in Wales. It had complex multinational connections: it flew a Liberian flag; its owner was based in Bermuda but was a subsidiary of an American company; it had been chartered by British Petroleum (BP); and its master was an Italian, Pastrengo Rugiati.

The tanker ran from the Canary Islands towards the Scilly Isles on autopilot. As the ship neared the UK, Captain Rugiati decided to go east of the Scillies but he was unfamiliar with the waters and in particular the Seven Stones reef which lay ahead. At just before 9am on 18 March 1967 *Torrey Canyon* struck the rocks, rupturing many of its oil storage tanks. Fortunately, the crew were able to abandon ship without loss of life, but the oil spill was the worst in history at the time.

The UK had no experience of how to handle an oil spill of this magnitude. It was decided to spray the oil spill with detergents to try to disperse it, and tens of thousands of gallons were deployed from an armada of ships. Once the ship began to break up, the tanker was bombed by the RAF to try to set fire to the oil but with limited success. Despite these efforts, a 'black tide' coated the coasts of Cornwall, the Scillies, Guernsey and Brittany.

Oil tanker disasters result in thousands of seabirds being smothered in oil and dying. They often drown, starve, are poisoned or die of hypothermia. However, this immediate, distressing, impact is not the end of the story.

Oil and detergents enter the food chain and later kill many birds and other creatures, such as the guillemot shown on the previous page, via an accumulation of these poisons in their diet. The seas, the shoreline and their wildlife populations take a long time to recover.

However, at least partly because of the *Torrey Canyon* tragedy, oil transport at sea has become safer. Changes in liability, ship design and international law have made oil tankers less prone to causing spills, and there is now greater expertise in dealing with them. Nonetheless, thousands of birds still die every year due to the effects of oil spills caused by tankers, oil rigs, old wrecks, pipelines and storage facilities.

It is estimated that 30,000 seabirds died subsequent to the *Torrey Canyon* oilspill.

95

Memorial sculpture and gardens

Commemorating the crew of MV Derbyshire, *the largest British-registered vessel ever lost at sea*

Modern cargo ships can be extremely large, but size is not necessarily a protection against the most violent weather. In July 1980 MV *Derbyshire*, a bulk carrier, set sail from Canada to Japan. It was a big ship of 160,000 tonnes and was carrying a heavy cargo of iron ore. On board were forty-two crewmembers and two of their wives. The last known radio message from the crew, on 9 September, reported being caught up in Typhoon Orchid in the South China Sea. After this, nothing further was heard, and there was no distress call.

A search for the ship was called off on 21 September without any remains of the ship being found. The families were devastated and sought an official inquiry. Although repeatedly rebuffed, they were very persistent, especially when sister ships of *Derbyshire* developed significant structural faults. A book was written about the ship's loss, there was a television programme, an active local MP and unions, and a petition to the House of Commons. This publicity and the potential safety concerns prompted the International Transport Federation to pay for a search for the wreck

Cargo ships can be very large.

which began in 1994 – fourteen years after the ship had been lost.

Underwater targets located about 2½ miles down in the Pacific were identified as the ship, and this persuaded the UK government, with EU support, to commence its own expedition. In 1997–98 a detailed deep sea survey was undertaken which filmed the wreckage. Collation of all the material took some time, but it became apparent that *Derbyshire* had foundered due to a hatch on the foredeck failing and allowing water in.

Initial analysis suggested this was because the crew had not secured it properly, but expert assessment soon revealed the true cause: it had not been strong enough to withstand the colossal pounding received from the huge waves generated by the typhoon. Water had initially entered the hold via damaged pipes, causing

the bows to dip, and once the first hatch failed, the sea gushed in, causing the ship's bows to dip further. This brought the next hatch under pressure so that it also broke and this seems to have continued along the length of the ship, with each breakage allowing more and more water into the hold until eventually the ship sank.

It took more than twenty years to determine the real explanation for the sinking, thanks to the tenacity of the Derbyshire Family Association. The final report led to a number of safety recommendations, many of which were adopted internationally.

The image shown on the previous page is of the memorial sculpture and gardens dedicated to the crew of MV *Derbyshire* in Liverpool, its home port. The photograph was taken the day after its dedication in September 2018, and includes floral tributes left by family members and friends.

96

A Falkland Islands memorial

A tribute to the crew of HMS Sheffield, *sunk by an Argentinian missile in 1982*

A fleet of ships sailed to the Falkland Islands in 1982 to respond to the Argentinian invasion of this British Overseas Territory. The destroyer HMS *Sheffield* had a crew of 268, and on 4 May it was attacked while engaged in a scouting mission. Two Exocet missiles were fired from Argentine Super Étendard fighter bombers; one missed, but the other penetrated deep into the ship, where it exploded and started a fire. The crew fought the flames for a few hours, but the toxic smoke and the potential for further explosions soon made the vessel uninhabitable and they were forced to abandon ship. Twenty men were killed as a result of the attack and its aftermath.

Sheffield did not sink immediately. It burned for two days, then was later taken in tow with the intention of removing it from the theatre of conflict known as the Total Exclusion Zone, but in heavy seas it started to take on water. Six days after it was hit, on 10 May, *Sheffield* sank – the first Royal Navy ship sunk in action since the Second World War.

The attack on *Sheffield* was a swift Argentinian reprisal for the sinking of its cruiser *General Belgrano* by a British submarine the day before. It had been initially anticipated by some observers that the arrival of the British task force might have acted as a trigger for renewed negotiations about the 'Falklands Crisis'. However, with lives lost on both sides, a war became inevitable.

Sheffield was the first of four Royal Navy warships to be destroyed in the Falklands War: HMS *Ardent* and HMS *Antelope* were frigates, and HMS *Coventry* a destroyer. In addition, the Royal Fleet Auxiliary vessel *Sir Galahad* was bombed, as was the requisitioned container ship *Atlantic Conveyor*. All six losses were caused by missiles or bombs from Argentinian aircraft.

An inquiry into the loss of *Sheffield*, which only became available publicly in full thirty-five years later, was critical. It showed that *Sheffield* and its crew were not ready to respond to an attack or deal with its aftermath. The captain was not called when the missile was spotted; the ship did not go to alert or turn towards the missile to reduce its size as a target; no attempt was made to deflect or shoot down the missile. When tackling the subsequent blaze, the crew's efforts were poorly coordinated, revealed deficiencies in training, and some fire-fighting equipment was inadequate. Certain officers' behaviour and knowledge fell short, and two were held guilty of negligence.

It was also noted that, at the time, submarines were perceived as a greater threat to Royal Navy vessels at the Falklands than aircraft because the Argentinian mainland was so far away. However, Argentine planes were able to refuel mid-journey and thus reach their targets.

97

Newspaper headlines of a ferry disaster

Media announcements of deaths on Herald of Free Enterprise *shocked the nation*

Before the completion of the Channel Tunnel in 1994, ferries were the most popular way to take a holiday or shopping trip to the continent of Europe from the UK. *Herald of Free Enterprise* was a roll-on roll-off ferry, meaning that cars and lorries could drive on and off the ferry via the bow doors. On 6 March 1987 the ship was taking passengers, vehicles and cargo from Zeebrugge in Belgium to Dover. The ferry was not full, but most of the 459 passengers were UK residents returning home. There was a crew of eighty.

Shortly after departing Zeebrugge at about 7pm, *Herald of Free Enterprise* began to list. The bow doors had been left open and as the vessel accelerated, seawater poured into the car deck, rendering the ferry unstable. Within minutes the ship flooded and capsized. Fortunately, it rolled over onto its port side and came to rest on a large sandbank in the harbour. Had the disaster happened in a different location, the ship could have been completely immersed beneath the waves, killing even more people.

The whole sequence of events happened so quickly – within 90 seconds – that there was no time to send a distress call, lower the lifeboats, supervise an evacuation or even issue lifejackets. The ferry lay on the sandbank with all its lights out, less than 100 metres from the shore. Terrified passengers were faced with escaping from a ship with an unfamiliar layout, orientated at a bizarre angle, and in the dark. Many people smashed windows and climbed out on to the side of the ship to await recovery; others had to jump overboard into freezing water. Many more were trapped below decks.

Rescue helicopters were despatched, and Dutch and Belgian vessels assisted with saving lives and transferring survivors to shore. In all, 193 people died, and anxious families had to wait hours to discover if their loved ones had survived or not.

Reports of the disaster elicited shock in the UK. In the era before the internet, hard copies of newspapers were still widely purchased on a daily basis. Most of the crew came from Kent, and the *East Kent Mercury*'s front page describes how 'almost every town and village is mourning the loss of someone known to it'. Many of the national newspapers, such as the *Daily Mail*, described how *Herald of Free Enterprise* became a tomb for its poor victims. At the time of going to press on the morning of the disaster there were twenty-nine confirmed deaths and 231 missing, but many of these were soon found.

A subsequent inquiry concluded that the bow doors had been left open by the assistant boatswain who had fallen asleep, and that the ballast tanks were still filled with water at departure so that the ferry rode low in the sea. Senior officers and the ship's owners were criticised, and new safety rules were later brought into force.

98

Two London bridges

Marchioness sank on the Thames between Southwark Bridge and
Cannon Street Railway Bridge

Antonio de Vasconcellos was celebrating his 26th birthday, and to mark the occasion a friend had hired a river Thames pleasure boat called *Marchioness*. It was a historic vessel. Built in 1923, it had assisted in the wartime evacuation of Dunkirk in 1940. There were about 130 people aboard *Marchioness* when it sailed from Embankment Pier on a warm night at a little before 1.30am on 20 August 1989. This figure included two members of crew and two bar staff.

As the party on board began, *Marchioness* sailed slowly down the Thames – first under Waterloo Bridge, then Blackfriars, and finally Southwark Bridge. Yet before it could complete the very short distance to Cannon Street Railway Bridge, *Marchioness* was suddenly struck twice in the darkness by a heavy dredger, *Bowbelle*, which was also heading down river. Neither vessel had been keeping a proper look-out.

The lower deck was flooded within seconds, trapping many people there. The lights went out too, which would have been disorientating and made it hard for partygoers to find exits or safety equipment such as life-rafts. *Marchioness* sank with alarming speed and those fortunate enough

to escape were left struggling in the tidal waters of the Thames at night in their party clothes.

After the collision *Bowbelle* did not stop, nor deploy the flotation devices it had on board, nor help with the rescue. However, people on a second pleasure cruiser nearby, *Hurlingham*, witnessed the events with horror and this vessel rushed to the aid of people in the water, managing to pick up many. Emergency services became involved but it was soon apparent that, sadly, many passengers were missing. A total of fifty-one people died, including the birthday celebrant Antonio de Vasconcellos, together with his brother Domingos.

The 'Marchioness Disaster' devastated the victims' families and distressed the nation, and there was a series of inquests and inquiries.

The report by Lord Justice Clarke, published in 2001, made many recommendations for improving river safety, and some of these were implemented. In 2002 the RNLI established four lifeboat stations on the Thames and their value has surpassed expectation. By 2019 they had launched lifeboats 14,096 times, saving 580 lives and helping 4,994 people.

A large black stone memorial was installed in nearby Southwark Cathedral, just a few hundred feet from where the tragedy took place, helping to ensure that the victims of the disaster will never be forgotten. It is a simple yet touching testament bearing the inscription: 'Many waters cannot quench love.' Poignantly, it lists the ages as well as the names of all the victims – thirty-five of them were in their twenties, while four were still teenagers.

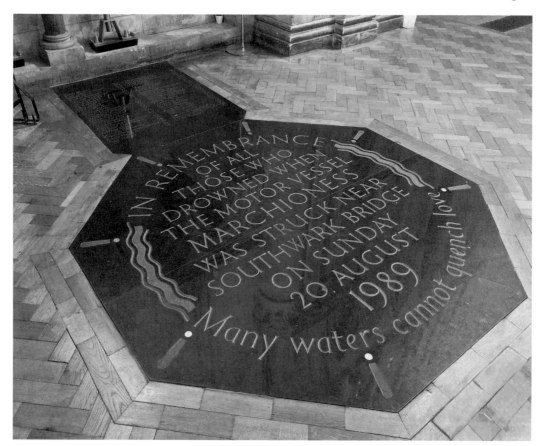

The *Marchioness* memorial in Southwark. Cathedral.

99

RNLI sculpture

Unveiled in 2009, the memorial honours those who have lost their lives in the lifeboat service

This impressive structure near the RNLI headquarters in Poole, Dorset, bears testament to the brave volunteers who have died trying to save others. The metal figures show one person in a boat saving another from the water. Around the edifice are the inspiring words of RNLI founder Sir William Hillary: 'With courage, nothing is impossible.' The memorial lists every person killed in the service of the organisation, as well as individuals who died trying to save others before the creation of the RNLI or in rescue operations that were not under its auspice. There are more than eight hundred names.

There have been many tragic losses of life associated with the lifeboat service. Some have sadly involved the deaths of whole lifeboat crews. In 1981 the Penlee lifeboat *Solomon Browne* from Cornwall set out to save the crew of MV *Union Star*, a ship with failed engines that was drifting close to shore in severe weather. With exemplary courage the lifeboat took on board four crewmen

despite 60-foot breakers. However, shortly afterwards both *Union Star* and the lifeboat were lost, carrying sixteen people to their deaths. It was just before Christmas.

In the run-up to Christmas 1886 came the UK's worst lifeboat disaster in terms of the number of lives lost. The crew of the Southport lifeboat in Lancashire launched in response to distress flares from the barque *Mexico*. Just as they reached the ship a huge wave broke over the lifeboat and sank it. When it rose again it was upside-down and some of the crew were trapped beneath. Only two of them managed to escape and swim to shore. The neighbouring St Anne's lifeboat also launched and when part-way to the wreck it too succumbed to the ferocious conditions, and this time every member of the crew was lost. In all, twenty-seven lifeboatmen died. *Mexico*'s twelve-man crew were eventually saved by a third lifeboat launched from Lytham.

In 1880 the small town of Wells-next-the-Sea in Norfolk lost eleven lifeboatmen. The brig *Ocean Queen* was driven ashore in a gale and its crew were trapped. The lifeboat could not get

close enough to assist so turned for home, but a wave crashed over the lifeboat and capsized it so that all but two of the crew drowned. Ironically, the crew of *Ocean Queen* were able to walk ashore the next morning after the gale had subsided.

All of these deceased lifeboat crewmembers and hundreds of others are commemorated on the RNLI memorial. It is very moving to see and read their names, particular when one considers that they were all volunteers. They didn't have to go out in the lifeboat; they *chose* to risk their lives for others.

The lifeboat memorial at Wells-next-the-Sea.

100

Two Titanic *museums*

Both opened in 2012 in cities intimately linked to the disaster

It seems fitting to conclude this book with a chapter devoted to the most famous shipwreck in the world: *Titanic*. The year 2012 marked the centenary of the great liner's demise on 15 April 1912, an event which has earned an ineradicable place in history. To commemorate this anniversary, new museums were opened in each of the cities which have the closest association with the White Star Line's infamous tragedy.

'Titanic Belfast' opened on 31 March 2012, as the cultural hub of the city's urban waterfront regeneration project. This whole area is now known as the Titanic Quarter and occupies the heritage site where RMS *Titanic* was designed and built. The iconic building shown here was designed to incorporate a range of maritime metaphors, including a star-shaped plan reminiscent of the White Star logo and the sharp angles of a ship's bows. The aluminium cladding is suggestive of choppy water or even an iceberg. The interior space is very large and explains how *Titanic* was built, including a shipyard ride; there is an underwater exploration theatre, and recreations of parts of the ship's interior.

Not to be outdone, *Titanic*'s other metropolitan soul mate, Southampton, opened its own museum called 'Sea City' on 10 April 2012, one

Sea City in Southampton.

hundred years to the day since the liner left the city on its doomed maiden voyage.

Sea City was created by adapting and enlarging the existing magistrates court and police station. It tells the story of *Titanic*'s crew, since the majority haled from Southampton. There are audio recordings from many of the survivors, and an opportunity to stand on the bridge and steer *Titanic* down Southampton Water and into the Solent. The original court room hosts an audiovisual display related to the British inquiry into the loss of the ship.

It is difficult to determine why *Titanic* continues to hold such allure. There are tragedies involving bigger ships, with larger death tolls, and of debatably greater historical importance. A huge number of shipwrecks have at least equally poignant stories to tell of death and survival.

The sinking of *Titanic* came at the beginning of the era of modern media; indeed, the first movie about the disaster was released less than a month after the event and starred one of the survivors. It is the media that has sustained our interest. Although eclipsed by two world wars, *Titanic* has repeatedly burst forth with numerous movies, books, documentaries, newspaper articles and websites; some survivors became celebrities.

Whenever *Titanic* seems about to fade from our lives, it bounces back: new stories, approaches, details, and of course the exciting discovery of the wreck itself by Robert Ballard and colleagues in 1985. Hopefully, in this book I have introduced you to some other shipwrecks that have different tales to tell, and perhaps you will be stimulated to explore them further.

Index